HOW TO GET ANYTHING YOU WANT

A GOAL-SETTING PLAN FOR SUCCESSFUL WOMEN
THAT WANT IT ALL, TO WIN IN LIFE & BUSINESS

THEE AMBITIOUS WOMAN

CONTENTS

PREFACE

If you're here, you're probably just like me—ambitious, determined, and passionate.

This type of DNA was ingrained in us even when we were young. Always striving to do more, be better. *We can call this the ambitious woman's DNA.*

Now let's rewind a little bit and talk about how this all started.

When you were a college student, you probably naturally had a single-minded focus. Your sole and all-consuming goal was: *Rack up those A's*.

When you left college, you remained ambitious, but now the focus is on your career. Instead of aiming for straight A's, your ambition was focused on developing the different layers of yourself in the *real business* world. But that's not it, you also became consciously aware that you now play multiple roles in life. You are no longer just the student racing after those "A" letter grades. You are no longer that energetic 18-year-old who could stay up studying, pull casual all-nighters, go to bed whenever you wanted to, eat a granola bar for dinner, or heck even sometimes skip your meals. You can't do any of that because you might now be a loyal girlfriend or partner to a wonderful man whom you really love. You might also be the dedicated home chef and cleaner. Not to mention, you're also the sister, daughter, plus a loyal friend to probably a number of terrific people.

You by no means have the intention of resisting or slacking on any of those roles that gave your life such a richness. Nonetheless, there comes a time when you start feeling stuck and frustrated with yourself. That ambitious woman's mind of yours starts spinning and spinning. It was telling you that there were so many things you wanted to accomplish, but it doesn't feel like there's an easy way to get through it all ? The more you pondered, the more it felt like you have to make sacrifices in one part of your life to achieve a goal in another part... How could that be fair? Why can't you achieve it all?

Just like you, like all of us, I went through the same cycle, which leads me to a conversation I had with my mentor who also felt the same way.

Gianna* is 30, runs a successful coaching business, married, and has two little boys. During our monthly catch up calls, we sometimes talk about life and I often asked her how she does it. How does she juggle all her roles and time commitments? She would tell me, "I'm not perfect! There are weeks where things are going great, and there are also weeks where you just want to blow the lid off the joint."

Gianna told me one way that helped her is joining different online communities for ambitious working women/entrepreneurs.

Women in the group were just like us....They expressed having too little time in the day for the things they needed to do. They would feel guilty about not meeting with friends or paying better attention to their kid or their boyfriend or husband. They had frequent emotional reactions to things going on in their job or in their own business. On the side, a few had health problems that were interfering with both personal life plans and focus at work. We're not the only ones going through these problems.. Thousands, if not even more, are going through the same thing.

One day I remember very vividly reading through a new post when another woman asked, "How is it possible for us ladies to be a great boss, girlfriend, and mother?" Someone replied, "Well, you *can't* have it all!"

And… **That** was the exact moment that inspired me to write this very book and the purpose behind ***Thee Ambitious Woman,*** *a productivity publishing brand aimed to help ambitious women to better manage their lives.* Because I want all the other amazing, motivated women in the world to know that:

You Can Have It All.
And Ambition Is Okay – If You Have a Plan.

It was from that day forward I became committed to find a way out. Why is it that we have to pick between keeping our ambitions versus having a life? Why can't we have both?

So here I am, putting all of this in writing. This is the plan that will help us truly have it all *(win in business & in life)*, without the guilt, stress, and constant self-doubt.

This was a plan designed from my experience, failing many times, but climbing back up and figuring out what went right and what went wrong. Learning from other women's experience, learning from my mentors, coaches, colleagues, and women who have "been there done that." This book is from all of us.

My name is Selina and I'm beyond thrilled to take you along this ride.

ONCE UPON A TIME

"What do you want to be when you grow up?"

Adults start asking us this when we are just little girls, and it is an often-repeated question. Here you are now, that grown-up adult, so answer that question right now. What did you want to be? Are you that? No? Ah, welcome to the club…

For our younger minds, that question implied that we need a goal in life. That we need a single, clear-cut destination or a purpose—or something is wrong with us. The whole concept becomes embedded in our young psyche. Anything embedded that young stays with us for a very long time, if not our whole lives.

Then we reach an age where we can make some of our own decisions—we have finally "grown up." For many of us that begins with our first job out of high school, or starting college and being in control of our lifestyle, study habits, and other kinds of choices. We are, albeit subconsciously, haunted by the need to have a purpose, to set a goal, to reach the goal… to know without a doubt "what we want to be when we grow up."

In our society, goals are a big deal. Goals help us get to "what we want to be when we grow up." But what goal? What *do* we want to be? And why are we so frustrated at the very question?

It is fine for us when we were little to say, "I wanna be a doctor... I wanna be a lawyer... I wanna be a singer... I wanna be an actress." The adults around us expected us to change our mind the very next time someone asked us the question. For a child not to know the answer in any kind of definitive way is accepted as normal.

But you're a grown-up now. What do you want to be? Are you being that?

In our society, that deceptive question, "What do you want to be when you grow up?" really is subconsciously pointing us to give a response about how we are going to earn money in the world, how we are going to make our way out in the world, how we are going to take care of ourselves as adults. And thus, embedded in our brain is that a goal is about earning money or learning something so that we can earn more money.

Business has latched onto this big time and made goals a very big deal indeed. You've probably heard of them all: SMART goals, OKRs, KPIs. They are all the same thing. Their intent is to do one thing and one thing only: to push us to earn more money for ourselves, our own businesses, or the companies we're working for.

We were never taught, as individuals with personal lives, to apply the same framework to areas outside of school or work. So we never learned how to set and achieve our personal life/internal well-being goals.

And here's the problem. Even though we have all these traditional frameworks set up that apply to schooling and business needs, we can't actually apply these methods to our personal well-being. Not all things in life are measurable or related to making X amount of money, or saving X amount of money to buy your new house, or losing X amount of weight before your wedding. Some of the most important parts of our lives are simply not measurable in that way. I think of things we dream of creating for ourselves such as our own emotional or mental health, our own unimpeachable happiness, positive outlook on life, or relationship with our spouse, our success at raising happy kids, or even how well we get along with other family members.

This is especially important for us women. We see ourselves very, very much as more than just an employee or business owner. We are very aware of all the hats we wear. We want to thrive and succeed as daughters, sisters, girlfriends, wives, lovers, mother, and more!

Your business might be booming, you've hit your annual business goals. Fine. But at what cost to your health and body? At what cost to your relationships with your boyfriend or husband?

Are you living a life that is out of kilter? You may not realize the imbalance or the consequences of that imbalance, but they are real.

Most of us don't know how to set or achieve goals for the *more important* intangible aspects of our lives that would bring everything back into equilibrium. We can't just work at SMART goals for everything in our lives. But... just because we lack the framework to set goals for our personal well-being, does that mean we can't do it?

No. In these pages, I will walk you through a new framework for goal setting and goal getting for us to achieve literally anything we want in life. Money, wealth, success, happiness, family, you name it. Say goodbye to your SMART goals, and welcome to this new era of goal setting.

How I Figured This Out

With goals being so prevalent and stress-inducing in the workplace, I felt out of place when I aimed, after work, to achieve personal goals with any kind of focus or measurable success. I got stuck in a rut and began to try to figure out how to have it all. Have it all? Sheesh, some days I felt like I didn't have any single little part of what I wanted...

Our ambitious woman's DNA wants us to have it all: a great relationship with our beloved boyfriends, time to learn new skills or passions, enough focus to maintain and enhance our bodies, and ability to hone our skills and awareness to become more successful. Our list goes on much longer, and this is where the pain hits: How was the traditional goal-getting process going to move me further in life?

Sure, increasing sales 15 percent this year will turn your business into a more successful company. Sure, as professional career woman, you get great satisfaction out of your professional pursuits. But what does any of that do for you in the greater scheme of your personal life and your "becoming" as a whole and complete person? Two things: Not. Much.

Those activities pay the bills, and I agree they can express some of our skills, talents, and passions, but they don't fill our *emotional* bank accounts.

After years of screwing up, random emotional breakdowns, going through countless cycles of intense work and then burning out, sacrificing my health and relationships with my loved ones, I finally have discovered a process that helped. It helped me fulfill my career and business goals, yes, but it also gave me a way to enhance my own personal well-being and relationship with my loved ones. At last, I finally felt calm, at ease, happy. Most importantly? I felt like I was finally living a life that I had control over. Wow! That was a reversal, and very welcomed indeed!

This all resulted from a simple shift in how I set my goals. Not just the ones we were taught in school or in our business. But goals that actually matter to us as a human being, goals that will enable us to live a balanced life.

The Yin and Yang of It All

It is a powerful cultural concept that can guide us in the way we need. It is the concept of yin and yang.

Yin and yang in Chinese philosophy illustrates that it is important to maintain a balance and harmony in ourselves, between ourselves and the world at large, and between ourselves and the universe. It is used throughout Asian culture, whether in traditional Chinese medicine, in adjusting the feng shui of your home, or in figuring out what is "going wrong" in your inner-being life.

It conveys the complicated dualities of life: cold/hot, night/day, weak/strong, light/dark, hard/soft. When the scales tip too much in one direction and stay there, this is seen as both undesirable and unsustainable over the long term.

It occurred to me that, just as we need dualities in life, we need yin and yang in the way we approach goals for our lives. We need balance among all the roles we play. We need balance between work/play, money/happiness, kids/adults, and on and on.

In short, I applied this element of duality to the way we set goals.

What we need Yin Goals and Yang Goals. How to set and achieve both kinds of goals is what you will learn about in this book.

You Can Have It All

Helping you have it all—*and* achieve a well-rounded, balanced life—matters deeply to me. What you're about to learn helped me get through the hurdles I called "*figuring out how to have it all without going nuts.*" I truly want to help you do the same.

This book is for you. The ambitious woman. The career-driven woman. The busy woman. The woman who wears so many hats in a day you need two closets for them. The woman who wants it all but has no idea how to get it all without risking it all.

If you are an ambitious woman, don't let anyone take that ambition away from you. Women of all generations, eras, and cultures have stepped up, followed their heart's desire, and made an impact. Look back in history, and you'll get confirmation that women (of all cultures) have not waited for an invitation to live out loud. Why should women of the 21st century be any different?

Go for it. Have it all. But be advised: You will always need some balance in your life so that you enjoy what you have created. What is the point of success when you don't have anyone else to share it with?

Now how can you get started?

Well, that's why you're here, and I'm beyond excited to share with you a process that will help you achieve just what you need.

I call this the *Yin-Yang Way of Goal Setting.*

COMPLIMENTARY WORKBOOK

If you're determined to get the most result from this book, there's something that will make your life so much easier.

I've created a 10-page+ fillable workbook which breaks down each step of this goal-setting process clearly and concisely.

The best way to consume this book is to fill out the workbook gradually as you are reading through the chapters. Don't worry, I've inserted action items or reminders throughout the book to inform you when to do so. At the end, when you are done reading the book, you'll have everything you need for **execution.**

You can scan the QR code (simply use your phone and take a picture of the code) or visit the link below to redeem your complimentary workbook:

https://theeambitiouswoman.com/goals-workbook/

(P.S: As a bonus gift for finishing this entire book, I've saved something special for you all the way at the end. Make sure you don't miss the final "You Can Have It All" chapter, there's a value-packed training program created for those that are committed to take action!)

Finally, let's get started?!

I

LET'S GET THINGS STRAIGHT

THE MOST POWERFUL GOALS ARE NOT FINITE

L adies, it's time for us to dive into ourselves and find out what brings us balance, happiness, joy, and fulfillment and allows our creativity to flow. That old James Brown song goes, "It's a man's world," and it has seemed to me to be true, at least as far as goal setting goes. But don't forget that the lyricist was no fool: Brown ends the song by crooning, "But it's nothing, nothing, nothing … without a woman or a girl."

As I have already said, there's a big problem when we try to follow goal-setting methods that are developed for the business world: It's hard to adapt them to the goals we have as women. It's hard to adapt them to any *personal* or *evolutionary* goals we might have. There is no guide to tell us how to achieve *balance* among all the hats we wear and among the facets of life that are important to us.

Vive La Difference!

Women need something different. Men know it. We know it. But men cannot devise a way for us to be fulfilled. We need to do it ourselves.

This book is about how to use **Yin and Yang goal setting** to make progress in all areas of your life as a woman. As an ambitious woman. An independent woman. A multi-talented woman. As a mother. As a woman with a professional career or a business to run. As a partner or spouse to a man who is just as great (but different!!) as you are. As a friend, sibling, daughter, auntie, sister… As a woman trying to do the best she can with her business, career, family, health, and wellness.

Yes, you've got some business goals, or just some goals about earning money and being independent in the world. So do I, and I get that.

But there is more for us than that! We females obviously also have different health and body concerns than men. "Surviving" menstrual periods during those long days in a classroom. Having a healthy pregnancy while keeping madwoman hours at work. Making our way through menopause without emotional/mental breakdowns. Staying attractive and sexy to our partner (and not feeling so exhausted that we become that cliché "not tonight, honey" person).

Men (yes, even male therapists and male doctors) will never relate to such issues, not really, because they'll never face them! We need to address them in our own way. But I noticed that classic goal setting doesn't seem to work on them…

As for me, I am a passionate author, coach, and doing all of this while working full time as a business analyst in a hectic tech startup. Beyond that, I have also discovered my inner passion for becoming an amazing home chef. I strive to be a caring partner to an amazing boyfriend, but also to be a great sister, a great friend, a trusted mentor, and a daughter that is attentive to my parents who gave me every opportunity to flourish. And someday, hopefully soon, I can proudly carry the role of a mother.

In short, I am *already* all of these women. I want to be all of these women. I want to fill all these roles in my life and value each one as it deserves.

Yet, as those roles layered themselves onto my life over the hours and days of each week, and as I got older, the more obligations I had taken on. That meant I had less time just for myself to be in a quiet space of doing nothing.

Just think about this, if you wake up at 5 every morning, work 9-5, come home to cook (and don't get me wrong, it had a relaxing effect), finish your chores, and wind up your "To Dos" by around 9-10 that evening. And then do it all again the next morning. Very paced and timed and scheduled.

Until everything fell apart.

You might relate to this as well. We feel "in control" when we know what we are supposed to be doing every minute. But we get weary. We start to think about the problem is that we are running in a race or marathon but we have no idea WHERE we were trying to run to. Where's our finish line? What would our gold medals be for? What would the outcome or result be of all of this very rote, planned work and "doing stuff" that we perform? And most importantly, at what cost?

Instead of making progress, I was feeling burnt out. I almost broke up with my partner. I gained 10 pounds in a short period of time. I was sad and stressed ALL the time. These were the failures I'm talking about. The things that no one likes to disclose, even behind close doors. But these were also the failures that helped me become who I am today, writing this all down to you. The good and the bad.

We Can Clean Up This Mess!

As a result, I have come to see that we are all in this mess of "unmanageable life" together. And my questions to you, ladies, are these:

What can you do to HAVE a life of your own creation and GET your life back under our control?
What is it that makes you happy, truly happy?

And again, to all you amazing women reading this, please understand that I'm definitely *not whining*. I was in the process (rather long, but I was new at all that stuff) of *identifying my actual problem.*

I have done so. And I think it is a problem we women all share:

We are going about setting and getting our goals all wrong.

We are so busy in our daily lives to the point that we've failed to really pause and ask ourselves what we are doing this all for. What is the ultimate destination we are all trying to reach? Yes, I believe in setting great goals. But if you do what I did and read all the goal-setting blogs, books, or YT videos you can find, you'll see that I'm right: *Our concerns as girls, women, and ambitious human beings are just not addressed in those success-oriented, corporate-ladder, be-a-winner-not-a-quitter materials.*

The Hoax

After this whole process, I realized that the way society (and by extension, business) has taught us to think about goals is in fact a hoax. Let's take a look at these examples:

- In **school**, we think of goals as "the letter grade" on our report card.
- In **business**, we think of goals as "revenue increases" or "percent improvement" related metrics.

In school and all the way through college, we've been taking what was taught when we were young to heart. We believe that the letter grade was all-important and meant you were "successful" in school, you were "smart," you were a "good kid," you were on the road to "making something of yourself." You got the grade you got. And done—finite goal reached. (But woe to us if mom and dad had expectations of straight As and we got mostly Bs... or worse.)

In the corporate world (most of the time)—goals are not something that are voted on but rather imposed. The executive management wants certain metrics to improve, or to reach higher revenues, or to expand into a new market with new products or services by a certain date. They impose those goals on us, and we as employees set out to reach those goals for them. We achieved the goal. And done—finite goal reached. (And again, woe on us if we or our team did not reach the sales goal amount, or finish the project by the goal date.)

First of all, both types of goals come from other people (school and management). Would you really, truly care what kind of grades you got if parents and competition from other students weren't big motivating factors to you? Nope. Would you really, truly buy into your company goals if you were not also making improvements in your own workplace skills and knowledge (and maybe earning a nice bonus for your hard work)? Again, nope. You would do things as your boss requests, but perhaps less wholeheartedly.

Second of all, those types of goals are finite. They are in a closed timeframe. But life is not! Our life is a constant evolution of becoming... We all have different roles to play in life; each of us wears many hats. The truth is that sometimes goals are going to be imposed. But personally, I started looking into goals so that I could fulfill the other personal areas of my life that I value, that I want to keep growing in.

For too many, a goal is done and they say, "Okay, next!" There is no link between goal #1 and goal #2. There is not much attention to thinking, "How did achieving this move me forward into becoming a better _____ in a continuous upward manner?" That is rather how I look at my goals now. I look at goals holistically and over a span of my lifetime.

The Crux of the Matter

In business, goals are about the numbers. These are all considered hard goals that are measurable and specific. When if you wanted to set goals such as become a better partner to your boyfriend/husband, to become more positive, increase your confidence level: what is the number that measures that goal achievement? Ah! There is no such number! The achievement of such "softer" types of goals needs to be evaluated in another way. But in what way? This book is my answer to how to measure our success in those *"soft"* goals that we as women need to combine with the more number-driven goals *(hard)* we might have. Something you will not find anywhere else, because it's only right here.

I see many women will only use goals in, say, their workplace or their own company because that is how business is run. But they won't head home and set personal improvement goals for the important other areas of their life.

Even when we were students, ask yourself about the push towards good grades, what happened when you finally got that A+? Where have you arrived? What better place do you live in now with that A+ grade? Does this A+ now mean you can slack off because you've made it?

Those types of get-the-A+ goals are finite in scope, for lack of a better word. We achieved X in Y amount of time. But I'm always stuck on my question, "And then what?" Did this goal #3 help move me into goal #4, knowing that the series of goals #1-#X will be making me...

- Happier in my own spirit
- A better person in relationships
- More fulfilled in my business
- Healthier over the long term

Instead, we should strive to look at goal setting as a holistic exercise, and that is where those "soft" goals have pride of place. There are so many other personal areas that we can improve on ourselves - mindset, confidence, happiness, and etc. **That's why the most powerful goals are actually not finite or measurable...**

The most powerful goals can not finite, because our potential as a human being is continuously evolving. Goals should have the ability to push you farther, farther than you could have ever imagined, once you do it right!

Not Once-and-Done

Where I'm headed with this is that improvement takes us towards mastery of tasks and skills, towards mastery of harmonious relationships... towards mastery of our life as a whole and complete creation of our own making!

Our results, gained from achieving soft goal after soft goal, are cumulative, infinite, and headed towards mastery. Only "headed toward" because I feel that absolute mastery is never achieved. Every master artisan (a so-named master at anything) will say, "I'm always working on it and improving," even to her last breath. Why then shouldn't it be true of the creation we call "our life"?

Say Bye to Workaholism

Friendly reminder: this new way of the yin and the yang is not about piling more work on yourself! We are, as a culture, already workaholics and don't need more of it. We always think we need to be working, scheduling every minute of the day and night, and feeling guilty on our rest days.

Just because our work or business is always in a constant go-go-go mode, doesn't mean our entire life has to be that way. Instead, take time to experience moments in life like the quiet joy of drinking a cup of tea from your balcony while watching the sunrise. These are the moments we need to appreciate.

You don't have time for that? The *Yin-Yang Way of Goal Setting* will make time for you.

2

WHY YOU SHOULD CARE

You might be asking yourself, "Why should I bother with goals? They have never panned out for me before. They always just seem to set me up for failure again." Well, you probably were doing it the wrong way.

Goals are not just busy work. Goals you achieve can create "I wanted this and got it!" and leave "I don't want this anymore" things behind for good... when you approach them in the best way for you. Goals can help you fulfill your potential, achieve your personal dreams, and create the best life experience you can have. But careful now, only if you do it the right way, the yin-yang way.

Often, and quite a surprising thing that will happen to you in this process is that a goal in one part of your life can give you benefits in an entirely different area of your life! This is the butterfly effect.

- Working on a body/health goal improves your *mental* clarity which you notice in your greater ease in your business.
- A goal about <u>cultivating patience</u> may actually give

you energy and fires up other interests in life rather than sapping it.

- A goal to read 15 minutes first thing in the morning can bring a calm, clear emotional balance to the whole of your day, making you the one who people start coming to when calm evaluation of a problem is urgently needed.

Amazing things occur when you set personal goals, but also when you personally set work goals. Just working toward such goals can help you improve specific work skills, bring you to working more efficiently and effectively at each task, and help you be the one to create more harmony in your business or team. It is, in the end, up to you to choose to set and get goals, even on the job.

Any long-term goal-setter might list the benefits she's gleaned, and it would be a long, long list! And let me remind you: The benefits of setting goals start rolling long before you achieve that end goal! Imagine starting a weight loss journey, and a few days in, you start sitting and walking with better posture. Posture? From weight loss? Who knew? You start on a new skill goal (example: copywriting), and just a couple of weeks into the study felt more self-confident. Self-confident? From learning copywriting? Who knew?

The more you work on your goals, you'll start to examine a long list of gains, that could be grouped into four major categories of benefits:

1. More **Energy**
2. Less Wasted **Time**
3. More **Money**
4. Improved **Health**

More Energy

Goal-oriented people seem to have a focus, a sort of mental filter that keeps the distractions of the world out as we work on the aspect of our goal that's important to us right now.

In other words, having a written, scheduled goal helps you stay focused in a highly distracting world. And we all know that it is a world where you have unlimited access to technology, but where you also have granted countless other individuals unlimited access to you via that technology. You've invited the world in to interrupt you… and forgot to close the door!

Don't forget that you are in charge of your own mental and physical filters! You may not realize that you can say no (or just say, "not right now") to any distraction or interruption that comes our way.

In other words, before I was setting goals, if my text messaging service beeped, I instantly picked up my phone to see who it was. If my email service beeped, likewise, I just had to read the email right away. As anyone as stressed out as I was can appreciate, that's a big drawback of having smartphones when you are short on available energy and focus. My parents, with a little smile on their faces, reminded me that all phones have voicemail. But my generation is not big on voicemail… we are a "gimme that now" generation and society (not to mention spoiled, spoiled, spoiled by the opulence of material things we have access to). Our attention span is a nanosecond! We feel that every connection is vital to jump on right then and there.

But my parents are right. Almost no connection is so important that you have to drop everything you're doing to see what's up.

In our day and age, distractions abound. Having a goal that you work on for a set period of time every day gives you focus to ignore the outside noise.

Having goals to focus on was not just energy saving but energy *creating!*

Less Wasted Time

The only person you are spending ALL your time with in this world is YOU. So ask yourself the question, "How am I spending that time of mine?"

You'll live 38 years or 66 years or 121 years. But during every one of those days in each one of those years, you will definitely have 24 hours that are—or should be—all yours. People in our society often think it's money that's limited, while others say it is our time on Earth. I'd state it differently:

It is how we spend the time given to us each day that is important.

In jobs, I get it: The boss is telling us how to spend those eight hours (remember though, that you are in charge of your attitude and work ethic). But what are we doing with our other 16 precious hours? And, back to that job, how are you approaching those eight work hours? What is their quality and effectiveness? I think all of us have witnessed workers who do the least possible work in the most possible time. Is that how your life develops fulfillment and value? Not mine! Even though the boss may ask for a certain task to be done, I try to focus on it to the exclusion of other distractions so that I can go to the boss and say, "Done. Here it is. I need more work."

In our home life, I get that electronics, TV, social media, and the internet are all ways we spend our down time. But I started examining that and realized it was not *advancing me* in any significant way to read Facebook posts or scroll mindlessly through YouTube. I was honest and saw clearly that it didn't relax me either. It was just another way that I wasted my time and checked out of my world, my personal intentions for improvement. It was a way I told myself that "I'm too busy to work on my business".

One minute spent is one minute lost from your life if it was not spent on good, valuable, fulfilling action. I'm definitely not telling you to schedule every minute! But I see that most of us look like we are running after a speeding car all the time.

Something like this could be helpful: At the end of a day, just lay down before sleep and run through these questions as you reflect on your day.

- Where did I avoid being the best me I could be?
- When did I literally say the words, "I won't work on XX goal today" and… not work on it?
- When did my self-talk get stuck in beating me up?
- And (this is usually hard by 10 p.m.) what did I achieve—not just do, but achieve—in each of my waking hours today?

If you can say, "I talked lovingly (respectfully, etc.) to __", or, "I helped __ get unstuck in that work project," or similar things, you know you achieved something. You connected with someone else in a meaningful way.

If you can say, "Yes, my love and I watched that new Netflix series, but we also snuggled, hit pause, and chatted, took our time to listen and be with each other," it speaks to your relationship goal getting some good air time!

If you can say, "I finished 2 sales call today and absolutely crushed it," it speaks to your increased self-confidence!

If you can say, "I ate healthy and mindfully today," it speaks to your health goals. And so on.

At the end of the day, this might be challenging, but then again, isn't every new habit and every new goal when you are starting out?

Wasting time, which gives you nothing in return in the long run? You'll find that you don't want that anymore, and you'll have tactics in place to not do it anymore. With goals to reach, you make the most out of your time every day. You not only do not waste time, it might feel like you've created time!

More Money

If you're reading this, you're probably old enough to understand that we all need money *management* goals rather than just *annual income goals.* On my first job, I was crazy from the fact that I now had "so much money"! Well, it wasn't all that much in the worldly scheme of things. I came quickly to see that money is a resource for me just as my energy and my 24 hours every day are important resources.

You'll start to realize that as you set meaningful goals for yourself (not about money but any goals) that your life as a whole will settle into higher energy, better use of time, and, as if by magic, a better use of your money resources.

I didn't at first set goals to manage money, yet my money fell into place more or less on its own. Money was no longer something I used to plug in the gaps of fulfillment I experienced before goal setting started. I stopped randomly going on Amazon to buy the newest kitchen appliances because I felt like "it would be cool to have in the kitchen." I stopped browsing on Lululemon because I felt like "new leggings would be nice."

Being focused on your goals will naturally lead you to spend less money overall, and specifically less money on things that did not contribute to your goals! You'll learn to focus all your resources—time, energy and money—on the goal at hand, and not frivolously spending money to fill a hole in your heart or tummy.From there, you might even realize that you in fact had a fair amount of unspent earnings.

What can you do with those earnings? For me, I set a multi-year goal to invest that spare cash smartly. Not having that amount of money in my wallet anymore was not an issue. I didn't need those frivolous purchases, and so the cash I used to waste on them was mine to invest and grow.

Improved Health

Body image is one of the biggest things a lot of us ladies tend to struggle with. This usually gets worse once stress kicks in and all that emotional eating comes into play… You'll start to see how multi-faceted the concept of "personal health and wellness" really is. It is about inner body, organic health, and not just being "disease-free." Outer fitness. Mental health and attitude. Emotional balance. It is about the sexual and sensual being that we are. It is about what we allow to enter our body: foods and drinks, certainly, but also doctor-prescribed medications, tobacco, and all that we might consider ingesting. Whew, that's a big deal to set goals for!

When you start to set goals and follow a goal-getting process, you'll actually learn how to take care of your own body. You can apply the goal-setting framework of which I will go over in the next few chapters to any of your health or body goals. But beyond body health, it'll teach you how to take care of my own mental and emotional health. Mentally and emotionally, you will no longer feel frantic, apathetic, or exhausted. You will no longer felt like I was on an emotional rollercoaster. Goals will give you direction. Goals will give you focus. Goals will give you the tools to take care of yourself.

You'll come to realize that you are no good to your clients, team, boss, coworkers, no good to my family or partner, and certainly no fun to be around with if you weren't feeling healthy and feeling well.

Past, Present, and Future

Goals are valuable. They teach us not only to be in the present moment but to also take into consideration what kind of future we are building, and they allow us to see and learn from our past.

Goals teach us to work in the present—to set smart goals, good goals, valuable goals, and to work towards their achievement—so that we can have a better future. They show us how to move beyond our past, since everything we've learned from the past (and the mistakes, failures, hardships, and embarrassments we've endured—and the pride and arrogance from past successes, too!) contributes to the new successes we have today... and then tomorrow.

You can only start right where you are in this moment:

- Some of you will probably decide that your health is in the toilet and it is time to take it into your own hands!

Well, then that is where you need to start with your goal setting and goal getting. Evaluate the strongest "I don't want" and turn it into what you do want. That is your goal.

- Some of you are perhaps too deep in financial debt for comfort. The debt is blocking your ability to own a home or condo, to really afford a safe vehicle or even to afford a family.

Well, then that is clearly where you must start. Evaluate the sharpest sticking point in your financial situation, that thing you most "don't want" and fix it with a new goal.

- Others have nothing but rocky relationships, with constant arguing, judgments, criticisms, breakups, makeups, and flare-ups. You also see they are giving you everything but a harmonious, mutually loving and supportive interaction.

Well, no secret then. You might as well start by evaluating how you can change that with a new goal.

My point is that we all have aspects of our lives we are really unhappy with, circumstances that *we just don't want anymore*:

Too little time to do things you love. Lack of sleep. Not enough time to hang out with kids. Not enough time to spend with your partner. Not eating healthy. Sucked into midnight sweets. Not enough skills to earn a living wage. Threats of divorce. No money. Blew off your education. Hate the commute. Hate your job.

If you are like me and everyone I've talked to, you know exactly what you want and do not want. And if you are still unconvinced, here is more of what women tell me they desire:

- Loving mother-children relationships. Are you spending enough quality time with your kids? Or are you constantly tired when they ask to hang out?
- Healthy partner/spouse relationship. Are you putting your relationship first or do you always sacrifice time for work?
- More confidence in their own bodies/self-image. That pesky eight pounds that just won't melt.

- Healthier meals, without feeling like they need to slave away in the kitchen 24/7.
- Hitting their sales quota at their jobs or work without having nightmares about it.
- Attain their own revenue goals for their business or side hustle.

You know without a doubt what you want and do not want. The solution is to identify what you do want and get it or get more of it, right? Goals are just the thing to get it for you!

There is one more type of benefit I noticed from working on one or more goals. I started feeling more self-confident, more purposeful. I started feeling happier! It was an inner-being benefit. And who knew?

My whole-person energy level is now at an optimal level almost all of the time. I used to get so drowsy in a typical mid-afternoon work day. It was the nod-off-and-snooze type of drowsy. If you also feel like this, that's most likely because you are doing things that you resisted or was reluctant about. Now, with the right goals, you will no longer feel like you need to say yes to everything and everyone—and when you say no, you don't feel guilty about it too!

No More Chasing Cars

One of my beloved college friends had many different roles in her life. She constantly felt like she was running out of time. She was like a dog chasing cars, she said—never willing to stop running but never catching the car! She'd get irregular sleep and call it "never enough rest," and frankly she always looked like a partier who fell asleep in full hair and makeup every morning. When liquor was involved, she'd overdrink because, "Hey, party time!" She knows the sleep issue is due to binge watching Netflix or her party-hearty attitude, but she just sticks with those habits anyway. She'd lose track of time and often be late for dates with friends, and worse, for engagements in business.

I think about her often. She was like the proverbial kid who didn't want to miss any of the action when mom and dad had dinner guests. Mom would put her to bed, but she'd sneak out to be with the party of adults until everyone went home. It is what I call the "don't wanna miss my life by sleeping through it all" thing. My friend acted similarly.

Does this story sound familiar? Does it remind you of how you were when you were back in high school or college? We often think of the past as the good old days. If we look back, though, and reflect on how we lived, we'd see that as a young person, all we cared about was our own present moment and our own instant gratification. Older now, our decisions are no longer just for us. Others are involved.

When we change hats and pivot into a different aspect of our life, we affect other people. Life gets more complicated, and that is just how it is. We need to wear multiple hats and that too is just how it is. But one thing still holds true despite anything else: we can be in control and take charge of the pivot, of the multiplicity and depth of our lives, and we can love every second with energy to spare!

The way of yin and yang goals will take you there.

3

GET CLARITY THIS WAY

Confused people don't achieve goals. Confused people (and let me admit that I've been one) don't know enough about the direction they want to go in life to get there. Eradicating confusion and moving into clarity is your next step.

Those things which are *important* to you—alongside those *beliefs that guide* all your decisions throughout your life—are called values. As the dictionary might say it, "values are a person's *principles* or *standards of behavior; one's judgment of what is important in life.*"

People talking in general about their values are not always clear on what they are or what is meant by a "value." When you probe others with some questions, you discover that their so-called values are just some vague airy-fairy type of feelings or a gut intuition about what is right. They really haven't worked at examining their values with enough clarity that they can write them down on paper in so many words. They don't own them.

Writing down your values forces you to be clear on what those values are.

I believe that many people have confusion about life in general because they have not gotten clear about what those values are *with precise, expressive words*. Thus, it has been impossible for them to line up their actions with their values and live them every day. It is a rare person who really sits down to write them out and ponder whether they are the ones that really resonate positively with her. When I say resonate, I mean with real energetic vibration. Each word we utter— each and every individual word!—has an energy, an energy vibration. That vibration can be low, heavy, and negative, or it can be a high, light, and positive vibe. Write out your values and you will discover, I believe, that those words have a light feeling to them. You have a deep sense of connection to them.

Just as I said with goal setting, it is only when you start writing out statements about "My Values" that you realize you were not as clear on them as you thought you were. It is nearly impossible to find words to write if you have just a vague feeling—and that is where most of us are concerning our values.

Though I have saved this topic until now, understanding your values is the most important step in effective goal setting. Seeing the goal behind the goal was one big step to clarity. Why? Because by going deeper, you notice that your real underlying goals are for changes or new things that are deeply *important* to you. Seeing the "why" behind any action must (I believe) bring you back to your values—to what is important, to your personal standards of behavior, to reflecting on what it is that must guide your every action… and to identifying what you really want.

You need to have clarity in your life, and knowing down deep, in no uncertain terms, what your values are gives you real clarity. From there, you can identify the precise goals that move you towards living those values more fully.

Examples of Values

Values are:

1. beliefs that guide you,
2. principles or standards of behavior, and
3. your judgment of what is important in life.

Translating Values to Action

What do values translate into out in the world? What could that look like?

Any of your values might lead you to a quiet, inner spiritual understanding that creates a comfortable yet flexible balance in all other aspects of your life and living.

Today, women have any number of challenges in staying the course, even after we have identified our most closely held values. Things have become especially interesting in this regard, as we're entering a new age of (even more) remote working and (even more widely used) distance learning due to the global COVID-19 pandemic. Your life is no longer separated by that "let me wind down" commute between office and home. Now your office, school, and home are all one place. There's no clear physical or emotional boundary or separation from your working-world hat, your spouse, lover, or mother hat, your run-the-household hat, and your daughter or sister hats. You are wearing all these hats at the same time in the same space throughout one long day and evening after the other.

I say this because of my own experience. I truly wanted to wear all those hats. I truly wanted to be all those women. I wanted to be every woman to those people and in all those circumstances. But I didn't have enough clarity to pull it off, even before COVID-19 threw a wrench into our separation of activities.

The more roles I took on in my life, the less clarity I had about my life as a whole. Can you relate? Juggling all those hats, events, interruptions, and needs alongside working a time-guzzling professional schedule didn't give me a moment to consider whether I was living according to my values or not. By the time each day was over, I did not even have the energy or the mental clarity to say, "I didn't allow myself a single five-minute period of quiet rebalancing time today..."

That is why clarity was my first step, and should be yours. I wound in and around that for a while. I knew that I needed to get clear about my values, what was important to me, and about my standards of behavior in the world and in myself in order to set any meaningful goals. I realized that no matter what goals I would set for myself, they would not have any positive effect if I didn't listen to my heart and soul about my values first. That is why your goals have to be in alignment with your own values, not just an expression of the wants and needs that you thought you had.

Discovering Your Values

I'll dive into the deep end of the pool and say this: A "value" is somewhat like our sexuality in that we do not choose it, but instead *discover* what it is. We do not pick it out of a list and adopt it, but instead we *awaken* to what it is.

Once we see that value X really resonates, we also understand our past choices and behaviors better! We *discover* that many of our behaviors, decisions, choices, and words arise because this value is activated within us. As an example, why is it that one person gets a bonus in December on the job and puts it straight into a retirement account, while another person gets a similar bonus and goes out and spends it all shopping for clothing for her kids? It's about the values that each one holds dear. The first person might have a value about taking care of her financial independence or abundance, as she never intends to marry or count on others for such needs. The second person has a value that puts family first; she has invested in her children and is buying things her children need.

Action item: Now is a good time to take out your workbook and fill out the very first step of this process! Let's do this thing together.

To discover your values, take the following step :

Step 1: Here's an example of the list of the most common core values. Feel free to do a quick Google search for additional values/words if you want to have other options, but I wanted to make this easier for you to get started quickly.

Abundance	Daring	Joy
Acceptance	Decisiveness	Kindness
Accountability	Dedication	Knowledge
Achievement	Empathy	Leadership
Adventure	Encouragement	Learning
Ambition	Enthusiasm	Love
Appreciation	Ethics	Loyalty
Autonomy	Excellence	Making a difference
Balance	Fairness	Mindfulness
Benevolence	Family	Motivation
Boldness	Friendships	Optimism
Brilliance	Flexibility	Open-mindedness
Calmness	Freedom	Passion
Caring	Fun	Personal
Charity	Generosity	Development
Cheerfulness	Grace	Proactive
Cleverness	Growth	Professionalism
Community	Flexibility	Quality
Commitment	Happiness	Safety
Compassion	Health	Security
Cooperation	Honesty	Service
Consistency	Humor	Spirituality
Contribution	Independence	Stability
Creativity	Innovation	Peace
Credibility	Inspiration	Power
Curiosity	Intelligence	Thoughtfulness

From this list, write down 8-10 values that resonate with you the most. Do not overthink this, simply select the words that feel like they are a big part of how you live your life and/or how you WANT to live your life.

A few tips to help you through the selection process:

- Which values can you relate to the most?
- How do I want to feel in life, and why?
- How will I finish the sentence, "More than anything, before I die, I want to be _____?" Say it out loud and fill in the blank.

Step 2: Group all similar values together from Step 1. Group them in a way that makes the most sense to you. There's no right or wrong way to do this, just go with what makes the most sense to you.

For example, here are the three groupings for the values I've selected:

Love	Inspiration	Abundance
Appreciation	Growth	Success
Empathy	Positivity	Power
Peace	Happiness	Freedom

Step 3: Circle one value/word from each grouping that you feel the most connected to. Again, there is no right or wrong answer; simply select the words that are right for you. I've bolded mine in this table: **Love, Growth, and Freedom.**

Love	Inspiration	Abundance
Appreciation	**Growth**	Success
Empathy	Positivity	Power
Peace	Happiness	**Freedom**

As a final test, ask yourself if these identified values make you feel more centered, more balanced, more "in yourself." If you didn't act from these values, would you feel less full and happy?

Matching Your Values to Goals

Now that you have defined your values, can you think of any major goals that you want to achieve in the next year that match or align with one of them? Think about everything we've talked about in the previous chapters. What are some areas of your life that are out of balance? Can you match those goals into one or more of your core values?

As an example from my own list:

My three core values = **love, growth**, **freedom**

- A goal that matches LOVE value: *to always prioritize and spend quality time with my boyfriend on the weekends*
- A goal that matches GROWTH value: *to become a confident and unstoppable boss*
- A goal that matches FREEDOM value: *to pay off my student loan balance (financial freedom)*

Notice how these goals don't have any dollar or number value attached? Don't worry, we will go through in detail how exactly to set these goals in a later chapter. This right here is simply to give you an example of goals matching to values.

This match brings me, above all, the balance and internal alignment I did not previously feel. It also provides me with self-motivation, internally-generated enthusiasm, and a sense of both personal and professional fulfillment!

When I first set out to create *Thee Ambitious Woman* as my self-owned business, I was pretty stuck and yet so very passionate about this vision of mine. It felt like everything I wanted, and while I still have my full-time day job, my books ultimately came first. I would work day and night, planning outlines, website design, logos. While I was physically tired, emotionally and mentally I was wide awake.

Although, it ended up turning into a toxic passion or toxic role for me as the CEO/author when I started neglecting my own personal relationships with my partner, my family, and my friends.

Eventually, this obsessiveness and grouchiness got to my partner, and sheesh, I mean, who can blame him? I was terrible to be around or talk to. We all have our dreams and passions, and being a little ambitious (I told myself) is never a bad thing. Why couldn't I just focus on what I wanted and have everyone leave me alone? I dreaded spending quality time with any one person. I was always too tired to do other activities. I dreaded every lunch and dinner time because I didn't want to cook (I used to love cooking!). With each of those dreaded activities, my head would scream at me, "But you don't have time!" I was a wreck every way you look at it. I was flushing my relationships, my sanity, and my personal well-being down the drain. Not for long though. I learned that I need to set goals for not only my passion in business but also my personal needs. I had to pay attention to all these areas that align with my values.

I do know we can have it all. It comes from balancing out the goals that align with your values and only focusing your time and attention to those things that matter. Now I know that and I know how to get it without imploding. But we need to manage it well or else it can be so overpowering that we become toxic… That's why it is so important to first establish clarity in knowing what the core values are that define you and how you want to live your life.

You might be scared that you are out of time. But what I found is even scarier. When you do have the time to hang out, the people who used to be there for you are no longer around. That's why it is so important to deeply understand your true values and know which things and people matter most to you. Knowing this helps you prioritize time and energy for them. And this is what we are doing from now on with our yin-yang way of goal setting, with each goal based on a clear understanding of our values so that we can live a well-balanced life. It is possible!

4

THE ONE TINY LITTLE WORD

You know that song about "money can't buy you love"? Goal getting can't make you happy. Not in and of itself. No matter how many goals you achieve, it won't happen... unless you are already happy now.

One Tiny Little Word

We are all pretty skilled at making excuses for ourselves and for our state of being. One way we do so is with the tiny two-letter word "*if*":

I will be happy *if*...

- I lose this last 15 pounds
- I win the lottery
- My divorce goes smoothly
- I find the man of my dreams
- I can afford to own a condo
- My student loan is finally paid off

This is a subtle, back-handed, sneaky way of saying you are not happy now. It is our way of making excuses to delay our unhappiness. Here are more ways we self-talk ourselves out of happiness:

- I will start my business if...
- I will learn a new language if...
- I will love my kids if... (And make no mistake, your children understand that there is a condition attached to you loving them or not. Don't do that!)
- I will buy a new car if...
- I will give them a helping hand only if...

The "If List" is endless! It is the way we make anything conditional. Conditionality is the way we get off the hook of doing or having or achieving or learning anything. The condition never seems to be met, so we are never ever happy.

Our subconscious mind loves it when we say the tiny word "if." That means it can commit sabotage to its heart content, in spite of your consciously stated goals.

By putting a condition on our happiness we are denying happiness to ourselves right now. We are shoving our potential happiness out into an uncertain future time.

Let me say this another way. If you are not happy now, achieving your audacious goals will not make you happy. Nope. Your life will not magically change after you hit goal #1, #2, or #3. Your life will not magically be happier in some future time (when you hit your goals) than it is today. Goals are not what make you happy. Let me tell you why, and it's a fairly big secret so read closely...

 Your mind gives you only *what you say you want*.

You are saying, "I *want* this goal, I *want* this lifestyle, I *want* this debt to go away," etc. You are also saying, "I'll do this or that *if* (whatever condition you name is met)…"

Ask yourself what the word "want" and the word "if" are telling your subconscious mind. The word want actually means "need, lack" and it also means "I don't have it now." It sounds far-fetched, but metaphysical experts and spiritual masters of all eras know that it is true: When you tell the mind, "I *don't have* $1,000,000," your mind actually hears, "Okay, boss, we get it—you don't have it. Fine. We're working hard to make sure that stays true." What? Yes, the mind will work to give you more of exactly what it hears you have expressed... which is <u>not having</u> $1,000,000! And you go round and round not having the thing.

In a similar way, in the "if" statements, the mind hears, "The condition is not met, okay, boss. We will continue not to meet the condition." What? Yes. When you state unequivocally that the condition is not met, what does the mind give you? A continuation of the condition <u>not being met</u>.

The mind is not your friend when you impose conditions and when you state, "I want/lack/need."

Sounds a bit convoluted, and bear with me for a few more pages, then go back and re-read this whole section. It is important for us to understand the mind and your self-talk so you don't sabotage yourself!

The subconscious doesn't filter. You say, "I want (lack) money," the mind believes you and says, "Okay, no money, coming right up! I'll keep on giving you that lack of money." You say, "I want (lack) more time in the day to get all my work done," likewise the mind says, "Okay, boss, no time, coming right up!"

Instead, just change that lacking or wanting word into a decision or choice. Say, "I *decide* to lose this weight, I *choose* to have enough money. I *choose to* make more time." The mind, listening to your decision and choice, says, "Okay, weight loss coming right up!" or, "Okay, enough money coming right up," or, "Great, more time coming your way." Only with the clear decision and intention does the mind start working with you instead of against you.

One more thing: Once we get whatever it is we say we want (Santa's Christmas gift that appeared under the tree, the birthday gift of our dreams, that nice big house we always wanted...), we get antsy. Maybe bored with the thing we got. Think of the garage, the attic, all the closets in your house, even that storage unit you rented. Aren't those places full of things you said you wanted? Sure. You bought or somehow acquired them, and then got bored or decided you really didn't want them after all.

The mind will get you coming and going, pushing to get a thing, then telling you, "Naw, you don't want *that*, let's move on because you know you want this other shiny new thing *over there.*"

That is what keeps us chasing after the next shiny thing! It's happened to me more than once, I must say. I thought that my life was going to change once I finished writing my first book. Instead of feeling proud and happy, it left me wanting more and more, thinking, "Come on, what's the next big thing I can chase, what's the next great book I can write?" It didn't stop with that "one thing I wanted" either. I was working so hard on my day job trying to get the next raise/promotion that I frankly don't even remember how I spent my personal time with my loved ones over that year. It's as if those memories were completely gone, wiped out because I was so focused on achieving that one career goal that I *wanted* so badly.

It is because of how the mind works, how our brains and bodies are never content, and how our successes are never ever enough that I got into using goals and a process to achieve them intentionally. I learned to celebrate the small wins along the way. I was truly happy the entire journey. The small wins made me feel proud of myself, and while I obviously would be extremely happy when I hit my big goals by the end of a year, I was happy thinking back on those mini-goal wins, too.

It is All a Decision

Using words like the conditional *if* or the lacking word of *want* (I lack this thing) expresses a decision if you think about it. But it is not a decision you'd like to really materialize! You need to be more careful in expressing your decisions, and keep in mind that the subconscious is always listening and ready to twist your intention into something quite different!

There is a thing in goals work called the *arrival fallacy*. I suffered from it—we all do. We have in our head that when we get our goal or fulfill that imposed condition that it will bring us fulfillment or satisfaction. We delude ourselves into thinking it will bring us happiness. But what happens in reality? We hit our annual revenue goals in our own business or company that we work for and we're happy for a moment or two, or even for a month. And then we find some other reason to disapprove and immediately chase after the next big goal. Can we hit $50,000 more next year? It doesn't ever stop... Our happiness was momentary and fleeting. Getting the goal didn't bring that lasting happiness after all. That is because we didn't yet know about those "soft" goals, the type of goals that are lifelong, evolving, or lifestyle-changing, inner-being awakening.

Start With Happiness

Instead of thinking that achieving a goal will make you happy, why don't you start with creating happiness first? Decide to be happy right now. Just state out loud, "I decide that I am happy now." What can the subconscious do with that, but give it to you! It'll say, "Right! Happiness, coming right up and we'll keep it coming, too."

I was participating in a six-day residential seminar a while ago with about 175 other people. It was a personal growth seminar, so people came to the event with all sorts of self-improvement goals in mind that they wanted to learn how to achieve. The facilitator had led us into understanding how the mind works to support or sabotage us in our goal getting. He had told us about avoiding the words "want, need, and lack" and substituting instead the words "choose or decide."

One of the participants had struggled with depression her whole life and had come to the seminar at age 23 desperate for a solution that was not about drugs or more years of therapy. As she put it, "I'm young, only 23. But 23 years of depression is a very, very long time indeed." At the end of the facilitator's presentation, she got up and defiantly asked him, "So you're saying all I need to do is *decide* to be happy and it will happen?" He assured her that it worked every time. He suggested that she just use "I decide to be happy now and always" as her mantra for the week and see what happened.

At the end of the week, she was the most joyous, laughter-filled, bubbly, and happily radiant person in the room. She never thought she could just decide to make such a change and it would happen (neither did the rest of us).

On the last day, she got up to speak. She said, "This week I realized that I was letting my mind boss me around. This week I realized that the mind was only going to be negative and sabotaging and keep me on a downward spiral unless I got back in charge of it. So every day, I did as you said and repeated my mantra over and over throughout the day. But I also gave other instructions to my mind with a second mantra: 'I am the boss of you and you must do as I say!' Before this week, I never realized what power I had to live a happy life."

The Right Way to Achieve a Goal

I made a decision. I decided that goals were going to be a fulfilling, lifelong adventure for me. If I'm doing this to better my life (and I actually am), I should enjoy the ride rather than hate every moment of it.

You need to start out with the decision to just be happy no matter what. Just sit quietly for a moment at intervals throughout the day and feel the happiness, the joy, the exuberance. I have done this, and you can conjure up out of thin air these feelings in your body and mind. Just do it.

Then you are in the right frame of mind to set some goals. When you think about it, how can you achieve any kind of valuable goal from a state of depression, negativity, disbelief, self-doubt, or disapproval of yourself? Start with not just positivity, but a firm decision to be happy... no matter what. Repeat that decision over and over to yourself as your mantra while you conjure up the feelings of joy, delight, and excitement in your body and mind.

This reminds me of a famous quote from Confucius who said, "We have two lives, and the second begins when we realize we only have one to live." *Decide* how you are going to live it!

Another decision you need to make is to let go of all the stress, guilt, and worries that you are not good enough, not working hard enough, not smart enough, etc. These are all toxic voices in our head that push us to take on more and more with no end in sight. Decide to enjoy the journey rather than delay happiness for every goal we reach.

Our highest goal is happiness and its achievement is an upward crescendo of more and more joy, happiness, delight, and self-awareness. Deciding to be happy is a lifelong endeavor, a continuous focus, and expanding your happiness to serve others can be a fulfilling experience.

If you struggle with happiness in your life (always filled with negative emotions), then make it a priority to go the way of the yin and the yang—choose "happiness" as one of your soft goals (as we will further elaborate in a few pages).

II

READY, SET, GO!

5

THE FOUR GOLDEN RULES

You are ambitious and have lots of ideas, dreams, and milestones you want to accomplish in life—I understand that, because I am the same way. You want it all. You can have what you aim for and focus upon. It is possible. The solution comes from how you set and attain your GOALS. You can use goals to get you to your desired future place or state. All you need now is a simple goal-setting map. We used to have one...

School's Approach

We benefited, without realizing it, from a great goal-setting "map" in our schooling. School provided a structure for us to achieve education goals when we were young, but just because our schooling stops after we reach a certain age, goals should not stop after graduation. Goal setting and goal getting is part of learning and becoming more of who you can be over all the years of your life.

Think back on your typical school year. When you studied American history, the first assumption of your teacher was that you knew nothing about this history. That meant the teacher was not going to test you on day one for knowledge you did not yet have. That "knowledge" was your big, audacious end goal, not your starting place. So, in school, teachers always evaluate what the class's starting place is.

Next, in middle school or high school, that American history class lasted the entire school year. That meant that the teacher could start with the beginnings of the American nation and take her time presenting the history in chunks over the weeks and months of the school year. In other words, she did not dump the entire American history textbook of 921 pages on you to read, understand, and be tested on in the first week of school.

A similar structure was used in all academic subjects you studied through high school, and then again through college. In college, the administration simply would not let you enroll in Chemistry 501 unless you had taken and passed Chemistry 101, 201, 301, and 401. Those four classes gave you the foundation in the subject; they provided the basic and more advanced knowledge you needed to follow along in Chemistry 501.

What the school educators were essentially doing for every student was setting a major goal. In middle school and high school, the goal was to understand a topic by the end of the school year, by breaking the subject down into bite-size chunks over the weeks and months of that school year. In college, the administration and the educators joined forces to create a similar learning structure. The major goal was to gain advanced knowledge of a subject. They arranged subject matter classes to go from no knowledge to advanced knowledge, with that major goal chunked down into Class 101, Class 102, etc., as a student progressed toward mastering the topic.

Not in School Anymore

If you are still in school, you are benefiting from a goal-getting structure, so go with it. Stay the course and you'll learn incrementally and get that degree.

But most of us are out of school and we are no longer immersed in the same type of structure and step-by-step guidance to achieving our goals. We don't have someone else's map anymore (unless we enter the corporate work world). That doesn't mean our personal goal-setting and goal-getting success stops cold—not by any means. Now, in fact, we can expand the types of goals we want to achieve since we are not so focused on academic learning alone.

There Is a Catch

Yes, you can expand the types of goals you set for yourself, but with a new sort of goal-setting focus. With this goal-setting map, you will be setting both yin and yang goals, or, in other words, *hard* and *soft* goals.

Every one of your goals can be classified as either a hard or soft goal. The beauty of setting these dual goals is that it brings you balance and harmony in life.

When we attempt to achieve a goal according to a process such as SMART goals (a method frequently used in school and the business world), we discover that the SMART process is not really adaptable to a soft goal. Let me break it down here.

Essentially, a hard goal is one that you can track in objective terms, through numeric measurements. For instance, a hard goal is to move yourself from $40,000 a year in personal income to $60,000 a year. You know you have reached the hard goal you set for yourself when the numbers on the page (and on your paycheck) reach $60,000. It's quite objective—no hedging, no fudging. You reached $60,000 or you did not. It is clear cut.

A soft goal, on the other hand, is harder, if not impossible, to track numerically. It is a goal for which no business-type numeric tracking will make sense. All tracking you do on these goals is subjective. Progress and goal achievement is what you feel or believe to be true rather than what any numbers tell you. So instead of calling it "tracking," I call it "assessing." It's all about intuition and knowing yourself from inside out.

Most of the processes used in the business world or in other goal-setting books don't pay much attention to soft goals as we will later fully define them. For an ambitious woman like you who wears many hats, *soft goals are essential to creating and perpetuating balance in your life as a whole.* You might perceive that some soft goals you set for yourself are the hardest ones to nail down and work on, much tougher than the hard goals. And that is why, in my view, it is so fulfilling to achieve them! Thus, my rule when deciding which goals to work on is:

Always be working on at least one soft (yin) goal!

Sounds Familiar

If you are in the corporate workplace and seeking a new position, a human resources manager will want to know which hard skills you bring to the job but also which soft skills you possess. Like our own soft (yin) and hard (yang) goals, soft skills are less readily measured with numbers than hard skills.

Hard skills for the workplace might include (and your level of skill is measured through testing):

- data analysis
- marketing tactics and techniques
- coding languages (SQL, Java, Python, etc.)

- project management
- MS Office software, where the criteria are "speed and accuracy"
- IT-related skills

Soft skills for the workplace may include:

- behavioral traits matched to the job (for example, attention to detail for an accounting position)
- teamwork (being able to work collaboratively with other people)
- leadership (able to influence team members/subordinates to do a job within a pre-determined timeframe)
- communication (verbal, body language, written)
- time management (able to deal with interruptions and still complete work as agreed)

Both categories of workplace skills are necessary to success-fully perform the job requirements; the two categories of skills allow us to not only work with self-confidence, but also with excellence and efficiency, not to mention making us eligible for promotion!

HERE IS WHAT NO ONE TELLS US:

*You need balance **in the kind of goals** you pursue. You need both yin and yang goals!*

Just as both hard and soft skills are necessary in work, they're vital to your personal life, too!

Working in tandem on personal hard goals and personal soft goals brings you a balance of skills, capabilities, qualities, and character traits applicable to your private life that parallel what human resources is seeking in their employees. Working on both types of goals (and we'll see in a minute what that means) brings a yin-yang balance to your life.

Thousands of self-help books on the market mimic business (hard) goal setting and goal getting, all the while having you work on soft goals with the same process and framework. Can you really SMART goals your way to live a better life? Can every personal goal really be specific and measurable? This is like mixing oil and water and expecting a smooth emulsion.

It doesn't work. Those books neglect the importance of soft goals and, more specifically, a proper way to achieve them. Soft goals are meant to impact our well-being and personal sense of fulfillment. By adhering to hard-goal processes, we might have an illusion of moving forward, but in fact, we'll just be running around in circles! Yes, you've successfully climbed up the ladder and got that huge bonus or promotion you were looking for, but in return, you fell ill and harmed your relationship with your family. That's still a success? Hard to call it that…

Success is often determined as doing well in business, acquiring wealth, or achieving a level of social status. While "making a certain amount of money" or climbing up to a certain status quo might be the objective for men, is it so for us women? Success for us is defined with a broader palette: being successful as a girlfriend, wife, mother, sister, and friend as well as being a great boss, manager, or employee is ultimately the true north star for us. You can be successful in so many more ways than business/money goals allow. Success doesn't always translate to just money value or your status quo—it's about your life as a whole and how successful you are in being the best you can be in the areas of your life or roles that you play.

To succeed in life, to find the true balance we all want as ambitious working women, mothers, entrepreneurs, wives, and lovers, we need to understand the importance of setting the all-important soft (yin) goals.

I'll show you how.

My simple 3 part **_goal-setting map_** will help you gain a level of real, goal-achieving success… without going back to school.

To succeed with this three-part map you must:

1. Clearly define your core values

2. Identify your goals

3. Plan to execute

In other words, this map will line up with your own core purpose, values, and desires for new future outcomes—and help you achieve your best year ever.

The Four Golden Rules:

After reading the next two chapters, you will also know which types of goals are hard (yang) goals—they are the objective, numerically measurable ones. You'll also know which goals are soft (yin) goals, where achievement is determined through subjective personal assessments.

You might have an inkling about that right now, but keep reading on because there are **four golden rules** to this unique goal-setting framework that you must apply when planning out your map!

I: Goal to Timeline

Raise your hand if you've personally set out any New Year's resolution and have 99 percent of time never hit those resolutions? Me!

Because no one wants to work on the exact same goal forever. One year is a pretty long time. Our brains aren't wired to think or act for the long future ahead. We care about the present moment, or at least close to the present.

That is where a 30, 60, and 90-day timeframe come into **play.** No one-year goals for you. Who can even think a year ahead? Not many of us, certainly. Life changes too much…

By setting only goals that you can achieve within 90 days, you can visualize the outcome clearly. At each 30-day period, you have specific things to do that move you towards that achievement at the end of the three months. More on this later.

II: Goal to Value

As you can see, the work we did on our core values in previous chapters will now come into play. You have identified your main three (or *core*) *values* as your most coveted and heartfelt ones.

Now using those three core values, it is time to clearly define a goal that you want to attain that will enhance and/or match with these core values in the next three-month period.

Thus, with three core values and one goal per value, you will be potentially working on three goals at any given time.

This said, the number of goals you want to set is totally up to you.

Your Success Formula: Always set one hard and one soft goal in any 90-day goal-getting period. In other words, at least one goal will be a "hard" goal and at least one goal will be a soft goal.

Make sure your top-most important values are truly the values you resonate with. Remember, values are a permanent part of ourselves. They lend a purpose to our lives.

III: Goal to Purpose

You now match each value-connected goal you have written to the purpose underlying it. This is the same as how each goal answers the question, "Why this goal? How come I want this? What is my ultimate reason for this goal?"

- Go to your list of goals and match every goal you have with the answer(s) to the question "Why this goal?" or its purpose for you.

To do this, you will need to think deeply about what you want to get out of this goal. Ask, "How will this help me grow… make my life better… help me reach my potential… make me feel fulfilled?"

It is the WHY behind the goal that will keep you motivated as the days and months bring you closer to its attainment. Thinking about the goal's ultimate purpose will keep you motivated. Even if you don't reach your goal, the simple fact of working toward it helps you improve and grow.

You will want to learn from your mistakes as you work towards each goal when you know it has a valuable purpose for you. You would easily quit without having a strong purpose.

IV: Goal to Effort

There's two kinds of people in the world: results-oriented and process–oriented. And guess what these big corporations and your boss values? You guessed it: results. I, too, as a business owner of my own brand, need to focus on results because how else will I know the company is progressing?

There're two extremes of the spectrum, and too much of either can have a negative impact on our lives. If you're solely focused on the result, you end up dreading the entire process or journey to get to that destination. Remember when we talked about "delaying happiness" in the first few chapters? Your entire vision is so focused on hitting results that you will lose any sense of happiness because you think you will be happy once you get there. Focusing purely on results is the biggest cause of burnouts or failures. Because the WHY is never powerful enough to keep you pushing. Results are merely a metric, number or dollar value at the end of the day.

There are also people who are opposed to setting goals and think we should not at all focus on the outcome. Instead, they believe we should just focus on improving our process/habits and that's all we need in life. Well, that's easy to say, but what if you're running your own business? How in the world are you supposed to track your annual profit, growth, revenue? Sure, waking up at 5 a.m. every day is probably improving my process, but how do I measure the impact it has on my business? We need some type of result (metric) to know where we are going.

Just like yin-yang, we need dualities in life. We need goals to move us forward, but we also need to improve our processes to keep improving. There's always a balance.

What I realized is that us ambitious women who want it all are never willing to settle for less. We can't focus on results solely because it will drive us nuts. But we also can't completely focus on habits because we need to have some type of metric to know how we are progressing forward.

Well, that's why you're here. I'm here to provide that solution for you.

The last key component of how to set the proper goals will use a combination of result and process, sort of. There's a grey line between these two elements that no one likes to talk about, and it is called "effort."

Yes, it is important for us to set a goal and have a clear metric of what we are trying to accomplish, but what we also need to consider is the EFFORT part.

Don't you hate that feeling when you've set out a goal a few months ago to make a certain amount of money and by the end of the month, you did not make the goal? The level of guilt, resentment, and frustration causes you to never want to set a big goal ever again. It brings us down.

By simply modifying our wording and adding "trying my best" before whatever goal you want to hit, you send the message that you value yourself and your success, for not JUST the results, but also for the amount of EFFORT (process, habits, routines, etc.) you put in. Yes, it might be sad if you didn't hit the goal, but did you try your best at hitting it? That's a question only you can answer for yourself. If you put in your best effort, then still count the goal as achieved.

If you let yourself enjoy the journey and not put yourself down, it keeps you motivated and will trigger you to work even harder the next time around. The level of guilt will fade away, and you will learn to appreciate this type of goal setting so much more.

I promise you, you will fall in love with setting goals after you take on this new perspective. This process will feel so uplifting because you will no longer be fearful of not hitting the goals you have set out.

This method was adopted from Stoicism. Now, I don't want to throw my philosophy nerd hat on, but one of the biggest things I learned from reading Stoicism teachings is that there are things in life of which we have 100 percent control, partial control, and no control at all. Our own eating habits we have 100 percent control of. The success of our business? Some people like to say 100 percent, do you think that's really true? The effort we put into our business is all under our control, but how the market perceives our products or services? Not so much. We can ensure the highest quality possible, but that doesn't guarantee everyone will love our products. We can't control the external circumstances, but what we can do is try our best and put in as much work possible to give us the best chances. That's why it is important for us to set goals to effort.

For example, you want to make $100k after six months of launching your business. Can you guarantee that will happen in half a year? Does your hard work guarantee that you will get rewarded in that specific timeframe? Eventually, but within that specific timeframe? Maybe yes, or maybe not. But one thing for sure: I bet you will work your butt off to TRY to make that goal become reality. And that's the power of combining goal to effort. Results are obviously important, but that does't mean we should completely despise our efforts behind achieving those results.

Bring it All Together

Now put it all together in one place, such as a chart or table like mine below. *Once you are sure whether it is a hard or soft goal*, you identify that in the table, too.

Let's see what my table might look like, below, for my own sets of goals:

Value: Freedom	**Goal**: <u>Trying my best</u> to pay off the rest of my $9k student loans. **HARD** GOAL	**Why**: So I can be closer and closer to becoming financially free, debt free, and free up the money to invest in other ways.
Value: Love	**Goal**: <u>Trying my best</u> to build a noticeably stronger relationship with my partner. **SOFT** GOAL	**Why**: So I can be a better, more supportive, more open partner with him. I love him and cherish the moments I have with him in my life.
Value: Growth	**Goal**: <u>Trying my best</u> to think more positively and more mindfully. **SOFT** GOAL	**Why**: Because I want to become stronger, healthier, and build my mental resilience. I can face all sorts of life challenges more readily.

Oftentimes, your goals could have whys or reasons that are very much alike, and that is totally fine! Your primary focus should be on the goal's true purpose to you, even if that purpose applies in some variation to two separate goals.

Action Item: Now, get back to your workbook, and fill out the next step "Define Your Goals And Why" section. You should have **1 hard** *and* **1 soft** *goal defined, as well as the* **whys** *behind those goals. Remember if you want to make the most out of this, it's not going to magically come from reading! You've got to take action, now.*

How Many Goals Should You Have?

We are ambitious women, and we want it all. Don't be fooled, however, into believing you must work on all your goals—all one hundred of them!—simultaneously. That's a recipe for going crazy and giving up on all the goals entirely. This said, also note that…

My "love" goal in the table above did NOT include all my relationships. One relationship with one person = one goal. Why? Each relationship has its own energy, its own needs.

My "freedom" goal likewise did NOT also include saving money for my own condo. Why? That is a separate goal from paying back my student loan. One money-related goal at a time.

I like to work on at least two but at most three audacious goals in each three-month period. For that timeframe, I will pick major, important goals that align with my values and are backed by my own strong why/purpose.

Often, when you feel like your life is out of balance, you may find that, for a while, you need to focus on one troubled area at a time. For instance, massive and focused work on…

- improving one particular relationship (Love)
- getting out of debt (Wealth; Freedom)
- improving your workplace skill set (Growth)
- growing your online business (Success)

That is totally fine, as long as you've identified the goals that match with your core values and what the why behind the goal is… then go for it.

It's time to ditch the traditional goal-setting method, ladies. Welcome to this new era of balance and harmony. Let's look at the next step to do in order to have it all…

6

ALL ABOUT HARD OR YANG GOALS

As I've discussed, a "hard" goal is not a goal that is difficult per se. Not in our case. Hard goals are simply those concrete measurable goals—goals you can track through numbers, primarily. You will know when you have reached it because the numbers match. You can track such goals through your own records of associated data and statistics.

Hard goals are measurable objectives and apply in your professional and personal life. You have a hard goal if it is about...

- Growing your business, such as generating a predetermined higher amount of annual revenues in your business or attracting a certain predetermined number of new customers—or both.
- Body weight adjustment, where success is reaching the desired weight gained/lost in the timeframe you set up.
- Career advancement in a salaried position, such as getting that bonus, coveted promotion, or desired

transfer, or completing some particular training making you more valuable to the company.

- Personal finances, such as getting out of school debt at an accelerated rate, saving enough to put on a down payment for a new car, new house, etc.
- Continuous learning, such as taking a workplace skills class or hitting the books to repass a professional license, getting your Master's degree, etc.

You see that these examples, although all yang or hard goals, are quite diverse. Professional or career goals, body goals, intellectual or learning goals, finance-related goals... they can all be hard goals for one reason and one reason only: because they are measurable.

Here are a few more samples of hard goals you might set for yourself:

- Your own business: increase sales revenue by X% or $XXX,000, get X number of new clients, sign up X more new customers on your training program, create a new product or service.
- Your salaried job: earn that $1,000 cash bonus at year-end, get a raise of 15% by the end of the year
- Personal financial: save a total of $XX,000 for a down payment for a new house/condo, pay off all your debt, whatever its source or type, spend $XXX less per year on eating out
- Health (body): get strong and be able to effortlessly lift your body weight or a portion of your own body weight, follow a professional training program and run a 5K, 10k, or a full marathon

As you see, each of these hard goals will require you to take specific, regular, recurring actions in order to achieve them.

Sometimes a change of personal or professional habits will be part of your process. You will always know when you have reached the goal because there is a number or something measurable to look at.

Hard goals, because of their obvious measurability, give us a fluid road map. We take a concrete and clear series of steps that build on each other. Our business and career goals probably all work like that.

Laying Out Your Hard (Yang) Goal Map

Now that you have your hard (yang) goal set in relation to a value and a purpose, let's get to the actions you will need to take to achieve them.

You will be breaking down or chunking down your goals so that they don't overwhelm you.

You will be thinking about and taking the proper goal-getting actions so that each day you are walking one step closer to your goal. How to break it down? The answer is simply a...

30-60-90-Day Plan

The 30-60-90-day plan gives you a breakdown for each month. Just as schools break down the massive subject of, say, chemistry, into quarterly classes over four years... just as businesses have three-month, six-month, one-year, and three-year business growth plans... you have a 30-60-90-day plan to reach your goals.

As I said earlier, our brain doesn't like to envision our life 12 months from now. It's really hard. Can we imagine what we are going to prepare for dinner tonight? Certainly. Can we imagine our schedule for six days from now on our weekend? Yes. Can we know that we will achieve some family plan by the end of this 30-day month? Naturally. Anything longer, though, is sort of hard for the mind to wrap itself around.

That is why I choose a 30, 60, and 90-day plan to help you reach each of your goals.

The table above shows you a sample of my own hard (yang) goal and my plan for achievement within a three-month period. This "freedom" goal of mine is "student loans payoff", so I can finally become debt-free.

VALUE: Freedom
GOAL: *Trying my best to pay off my remaining student loans $9k*

	Action Items
30-Day Plan	o Cancel entertainment - monthly subscriptions that are not heavily used o Cut out Amazon shopping for "wants" only necessities o Automate $2,000 of my monthly salary to student loan payment
60-Day Plan	PLAN ONCE 30 DAYS IS COMPLETE
90-Day Plan	PLAN ONCE 60 DAYS IS COMPLETE

You see that I don't achieve the goal in the first 30-day period, but I have some specific action items to perform by the end of that first month. I do the same things in month 2 while adding some new efforts, and repeat that approach in month 3.

That is a sample of an actual map that I planned in advance and that got me that extra cash needed to fully pay off the loan by Day 90. I had some recurring actions that I did consistently for the 30-60-90-day periods. That made the process feel like a flow. You don't need to feel like you need to reinvent the wheels every time. Then after 90 days, with no remaining loan balance, I had freed-up cash for my next big goal of investing my available cash for profit and for future needs. One goal rolls into the next.

Action Item: Now it's time to fill out your hard goal map in the workbook, and write down the key items you want to accomplish in the first 30 days to help you reach your goal.

THE BIG RULE:

Fill out your plan one month at a time.

What is really important is that you only plan out the action items one month at a time, only after that 30 days period, you then plan out the next 30 days. It's a continuation process where you keep improving yourself to get to that final goal of which you want to hit by the end of the 90 days period.

If you try to plan out everything for the entire three-month period, well that's probably a recipe for failure... I know because I've tried. I've created countless quarterly road maps or vision boards, not just for my own business but also in my day job. None of them—not a single one of them—was a success. It gave me great ideas and is inspiring when you first do it. But that's not enough. It's great to have a vision and have an idea of your annual goals, but what about your daily or weekly plans? Everyone likes to talk about the big end goal, the final destination, the dream, but no one likes to talk about the nitty gritty. Because it is not "exciting." In fact, it is boring because, yes, consistency is what gets us there, not the exciting dream we desire that we suddenly wake up to and have seemingly achieved overnight. There's only one scenario when that ever happens: those fantasy movies that we love. But wake up now hun, we're in reality, the real world.

There's also another problem of being too much of a "planner." Planning is needed, but there should be a balance in how far in advance and how much we plan in our lives. You can't possibly predict or anticipate everything to go according to plan. If that was the case, then everyone who set out their New Year's resolutions would hit them, right? Yep, exactly not. Beyond that, what excitement does that give us if we know exactly how our future will play out? Stop trying to plan your entire year. See it through a different lens by planning out things one month at a time. See how far life can take you to get to that one big goal. Leave some wiggle room for excitement or surprises in your journey, and that's what makes this **goal setting process** even more enjoyable.

By simply breaking out the goal into three actionable blocks of 30 days each and only planning one month at a time, your brain and mind will be much more motivated to take the action needed to get you closer to that goal. Yes, the dream or destination is amazing, but what gets you there ultimately is what you do in your daily life, the action items that you put in your monthly plan.

Remember, this is a "flexible" and "dynamic" approach to traditional goal-setting methods. This is something you will keep whether digitally on your laptop or in a notebook. But remember, the key is *you can always come back and modify the action plan*, whether it is adding more tasks you want to complete in those 30, 60, or 90 days, or if you need to eliminate one or more.

There's also a huge keyword that I hope you were able to spot: "**Trying my best**". Remember the last key rule we discussed in the last chapter? Goal to Effort. Your success vs failure is not determined on whether or not you hit the actual metrics, it is whether or not you tried your best in attaining that goal. You won't ever have to fear about "not hitting a goal", as long as you put in all your efforts, then you have nothing to worry about.

This type of goal-setting process will help you adapt to sudden changes or things that can get thrown at us in life. Yes, it is important that we stay committed to our goals, but we need to accept that the plan or action items could change from month to month. The way to get to our end goal is our ability to learn, to be able to pivot and be flexible to change. That is ultimate key to getting anything we want. To not be rigid and stubborn, but be willing to modify when needed.

I know you might be getting excited and want to get started right away, but please read on and finish the entire book before taking any action because I have something special for you at the very end of the book. I'm here to do the majority of the lifting, providing you the structure for success; the rest is up to you to take action and make the change you need in life. Now read on, because we're not even halfway through the ride…

7

ALL ABOUT SOFT OR YIN GOALS

Soft goals, contrasted with the hard goals described above, are not as easily measured in numbers or data. These goals need not be vague—far from it!—but it is simply difficult to assign an objective number that cries out, *"Goal achieved!"* You can, however, assign *subjective* criteria to them that will help you determine your degree of progress or achievement.

Let's first get clear on what an actual soft or yin goal might look like. You have a soft goal if you set out to...

- improve current relationships with family, spouse, or kids
- overcome money scarcity mindset
- think more positively
- mindfulness
- greater confidence
- become a happier person

Is the achievement or move toward your soft goals harder to measure? Yes. This is where "assessments" and "goal scores" come into the picture.

We'll look in a moment at a quick and easy way—with no fuss, no muss—at assessing your progress towards that soft goal as you do the pre-determined work or actions that get you there.

Yin or soft goals are more "touchy-feely" than hard ones. You can't really plan out a road map or, in other words, a "business plan" to soft goals, because achieving soft goals is often the result of the small things we do daily that add up to make us feel more whole and complete. They are more like pouring a glass of water, where every week you gradually pour more water into a big empty glass. Some weeks you might pour in a spoonful of water because that is all you "progressed" that week. Another week, you'll pour in a big hearty splash of water and feel like you are really making tracks to your big goal. No matter how much water you pour in, trust me, you will know when you've achieve your goal—your heart and soul will know.

Life is never truly predictable for us. It can throw curve balls. One day we are breaking down crying, and the next day we feel happy and delighted. Hormones, PMS, pregnancy, menopause—these are just a few of the irregularities of how our bodies function. But hey, that's why you set the soft goal in the first place, right? When life throws lemons at you, make lemonade. You can always make the best of your current situation with a positive attitude and "goal-getter" mindset.

Life will never be perfect, but with soft (yin) goals helping us become grounded and have a clear self-awareness, then that is as perfect as we can get.

Laying Out Your Soft (Yin) Goal Map

Let me repeat myself: Having a number of soft goals all the time is *just as important as* (or more important) than pursuing hard goals.

Now let's get to the actions you will need to take to achieve them. Step 2 in the Map is about taking action, and it applies to both hard and soft goals. However, keep in mind that your action items are going to somewhat different for hard and soft goals.

You will be thinking about and taking the proper goal-getting actions so that each day you are walking one step closer to your goal. How to break it down? The answer, again, is to create a 30-60-90-day plan.

30-60-90-Day Plan

For a soft or yin audacious goal, what you need to start with is a ***personal assessment***. Every 30 days you will be working toward an improvement in the startup assessment score.

Soft or Yin Goal Map

You will start Day 1 with a starting assessment score. That will be your baseline for your current soft goal, and at the end of the 90 days period you will give yourself a final score.

Your assessment score is a value between 0 and 10. Zero is the lowest you can score. Ten is the highest you can score.

You self-assess on Day 1 and Day 90. And don't worry if you think that your assessment score will be bias since you're doing it yourself. This is where we leverage the power of weekly reflection so you have actual content to judge your growth throughout this period. More on that in the next chapter!

You probably understand how this all works now since we just went over the hard goals, but to give you a clearer picture, I've included a table below for your own reference. The soft goal of "trying my best to increase my confidence level " aligns with the "Growth" value that was defined in the clarity chapter.

VALUE = Growth

GOAL = *Trying my best to increase my confidence level*

Day 1 Score: ___	**Action Items**
30-Day Plan	○ create a morning affirmation routine ○ skincare routine ○ create a list of my strengths and review it every day
60-Day Plan	PLAN ONCE 30 DAYS IS COMPLETE
90-Day Plan Final Score: ___	PLAN ONCE 60 DAYS IS COMPLETE

On Day 1, I perform a personal assessment of my starting point with my current confidence level on a scale of 0 to 10.

Please be aware that it does not matter at all what goal score you start with. If you have set this goal for yourself, you probably don't rate yourself very high. Your objective with such soft goals is only to increase that goal score over the three-month period.

For the 30-day period, if you've set a soft goal to boost your confidence level, here's what you might include in your action plan. It might include something like creating a powerful morning affirmation routine, skin care routine to boost your self-esteem, or even creating a list of your strengths and review that everyday. It doesn't matter what the items are, as long as it is supporting you in attaining that soft goal, then you're good to go.

Repeat this planning cycle for the next 2 months, but remember the key is <u>only plan your action items after each month is completed</u>! There's no need to do all of this planning in one sitting.

At the end of the 90 days period, you do a final self-assessment to see whether you have progressed all the way. You may consider your soft goal achieved if your final score has increased from Day 1 to Day 90 period.

Action Item: Fill out your soft goal map in the workbook, give yourself a starting assessment score, and write down the key items you want to accomplish in the first 30 days to help you reach your goal.

It's not a race, it's a lifelong marathon. Small steps are better than trying to do everything all at once. Also, don't feel like you need to reinvent the wheels to do something totally different the next month. I often include a few repeating action items in my plan because that's what has worked for me. How are the action items you are planning moving you closer to your soft goal? That's the key question you need to ask yourself during this planning process.

Your success or failure at achieving soft (yin) goals is determined by whether or not *you tried your best* (remember goal to effort?) to increase your own personal assessment score from its starting level. Effort and knowing your intuition is key here. No one else can give you a score better than you can.

You will know! A score is merely a number you write down at the end of the day. It is how you feel deep inside. You will be able to easily tell if you've achieved a change for the better.

But you won't be done. Soft (yin) goals are rarely once-and-done. Setting and working such a goal serves to awaken you to new needs, to help develop new habits and attitudes. Just keep on going love.

8

WRITE THOSE FEELINGS DOWN

This final—and really continuous—step of our goal setting map calls for quiet alone time to reflect.

This last step is about looking back on things, asking how you did and where you went wrong or got things right. This step is the same for both hard and soft goals.

By becoming a goal setter and a goal getter, you will be doing more and becoming more than you thought possible. You will be meeting challenges that you set for yourself—and looking at yourself in bemused amazement because you did it!

You *wrote out* your values, your big, audacious yin-yang goals, your whys, your 30-60-90-day plans with their action item lists, and I insisted that you do this for a reason: You now have tangible notes, words, scores, and pictures to remember what you did and reflect on how you have done.

Ask the same questions of yourself at the end of each week:

- How did I do balancing out my yin (soft) and yang (hard) goals?

- How can I come back to balance?
- What did I do well/achieve this past week?
- How did I fall short/not fulfill my own plan this past week?
- What were some of the biggest lessons I learned this week?

As you work through each 30-day period of any hard or soft goal, you will make mistakes, perhaps fail to perform your own listed action items, or just feel like throwing in the towel. *Write those feelings down.* Reflection is a crucial step, and as you look back on those notes about failures or resistance to moving ahead with your plan, what did you end up doing? Did you forge ahead or give up entirely?

This reflection happens at the end of the week, each month, and when all is said and done. See how well or poorly you did in accomplishing your goal. Any small wins are cause for celebration—and if you learned something about yourself that you love, great! If you learned something about yourself that you just don't want anymore, write a new goal.

As you reflect on the challenges you've met, the 30-day plans you wrote up, or action items you've completed (or did not), you learn about yourself. Your awareness may awaken in ways that are not apparently connected to the goal. Here is what I mean...

One of my good friends has run 5k races for several years in a row, several times a year. Her partner looked at her one day last year and asked her, "Why haven't you ever run a full marathon?" That became her new big, audacious goal: train for and complete her first full marathon.

Hard Goal Example

Because it was an apparently "physical" goal, she imagined that all her learning would be about her body. She was wrong! She learned that she had more stamina than she believed, yes, but that was mental stamina more than physical in her view. She had much stronger control over her negative self-talk than she ever imagined she would—and that, too, was all mental. Her negative mind would be telling her, "Your calves are going to explode. Stop running!" and other thoughts to make her quit for the day. She just sort of observed her mind each time and said, "Shut up," and kept running. She kept running no matter how her mind tried to shut her down, and no matter how her body groaned and creaked.

She followed her training regimen to the letter, meeting each mini-goal and performing each action item within that mini-goal. She increased the number of miles she could run comfortably according to the mini-goal she had set. A month before the marathon (and also according to mini-goal action items), she ran four once-weekly marathons on her own as a test.

Yes, she admitted to me that the test runs were grueling and took forever, but she completed all four of them. She was one of the first runners registered for the marathon; she ran the whole race and completed it honorably in the middle of the pack.

She certainly was learning a lot about her body's capacity to expand, endure, strengthen, heal, and adapt. But she said she learned more about her mental capabilities and resilience, how she had control over negative self-talk.

She imagined she'd be learning loads of new things only about her body, and she did. But what blew her away was the lesson that "everything is of the mind"!

 Moral of that story: *Sticking it out or quitting is a mental decision. Upping the ante and going for broke is*

> *a mental decision, just as lowering your standards to go
> for a lesser goal is a mental choice.*

Reflect on your own challenges as you work toward your big,
audacious hard goal and ask yourself what you have learned
about yourself. Are you, too, gaining control over the mental
noise while working a goal? Well, join the club. We all are!

Hard Goal Failure – Or Was It?

Reflection also asks you to look at the goals you did not have
any big wins for. Ask yourself what you learned and review
the progress you made in spite of not reaching the big, audacious goal. Here is what I mean:

A good friend and colleague of mine in the sales team was
challenged to move from $10M in sales revenue to $15M in
one year. Whew! They wrote up a mini goal-type plan and
listed out the overall team's and each salesperson's action
items, objectives, tactics, and strategies. They worked like
crazy people (but smart ones with a plan) all year. They fell
short… They only reached $13.5M in sales… And you know
what their direct boss and the company president did?
THEY CELEBRATED! Why, if the team had failed to
reach their goal? Because they'd still increased company
revenues quite dramatically, adding over 30 percent to the
business's gross revenues. And wasn't that the point?

 Moral of that story: *You can always find small
wins, even when you think you lost.*

Soft Goal Example

A common soft goal topic deals with relationships: friend-
ships, professional and community relationships,
parent/child relationships, spouse/partner relationships, and
so on. One such soft goal a friend of mine had was to

"become a more attentive wife to my spouse who has been feeling neglected." While this was similar to my own relationship goal (I kept my mouth shut!), she approached things differently. And that was totally great.

Her self-assessment score was a 3 on a scale of 10! That shocked her into action. But... what action? Since her spouse was intimately involved in this goal, she just decided to ask him straight out. It led to quite an interesting conversation, during which she took notes. She learned (had always really known) his three main points of contention—the sticking points about her behavior—that bothered him. Lastly, she had to get an initial assessment score about this issue from him. She held her breath... He gave her a 4.5 on a scale of 10.

She had to try really hard not to justify herself to him. She had to try just as hard not to rationalize her behaviors to herself! But her goal was attached to her core value of "marriage and family first," and to her purpose of "improving all long-term relationships," for her own comfort and ease and for the harmony that she and her spouse would share in the future.

She started brainstorming the small actions she could take on each point to improve his feeling of neglect by her. These were actions that had nothing directly to do with anything her spouse did. These were her own little "secret" actions (but how could her spouse not notice...?!) that she took every day. At the next 30-day assessment, it turned out he had noticed, and his score on that 0-10 scale for her inched up. For that assessment period, her score for herself was noticeably higher, but so was his! She kept going all the way until the end of the full three-month program. She was all in and fully focused, especially after the first assessment proved to her that he thought she was making progress in paying him more loving and focused attention.

Whether you are married or in a committed relationship or not, you must have noticed how much trust, openness, and respect these two individuals had for each other from the start. This is a good example of what soft goals are all about and how to measure progress in achieving them.

Soft Goal Success – But Are You Done?

In this soft goal example, we notice that there is no final destination. No absolutely final stopping point. Why is this? They didn't end up at a 10, first of all. There is always more and better we can do on soft goals! Because of the nature of relationships, and especially of long-term relationships, both people are continuously evolving as individuals and thus your relationship together likewise evolves overtime. This couple might have to go back to the drawing board and we will never know for what reason. Maybe they decide they want to have kids now. Maybe one has a parent who is terminally ill and requires a great deal of personalized attention. We never know what life will hold, and that is why soft goals are either continuous or periodically revisited.

Life won't be suddenly perfect after you finish your 30-60-90-day goals plan. Life is always throwing change at us. The important thing is that we're improving and able to adapt and adjust to those changes! As long as you stay true to your values, set the proper hard and soft goals matching up to your values, and have a clear purpose for that goal, you will thrive and flourish.

Throw Out the Old

It's time to ditch the old goal-setting method, ladies. We're no longer in the age of our moms and nannas where our only option is stay-at-home mom or homemaker. Yes, many of our traditional cultures would like it to be forever like the past. But you truly do have more opportunities than ever and it's possible to be fulfilled, thrive, and pursue your happiness.

Don't live according to other people's expectations—not your boss's, your dad's, or your culture's.

Create your beautiful life with balance and harmony. Have it all ways—yin and yang, soft goals and hard goals, busy schedule yet time for everything on it… because you have a cool head, purpose, are in charge, and going with your new flow.

You can be anything: the next manager, executive of your company, or the CEO of your own business; the respected and beloved girlfriend, spouse, mother, daughter, and sister; the talented designer or the local hair stylist. Work with your values, flow with your roles, know your purpose—thrive. I believe in you.

III

YOU ARE MORE THAN READY

9

THE 3FS: FLAWS, FEARS, AND FAILURES

E ver since we were young school kids, we've always looked at Fs as something fearsome. F for Fear! I was careful to never go there. I know there is a funny thing called the "Asian F" (it is an A-), but I don't think culture has anything to do with this more or less universal schoolchild fear.

As children, we also feared getting yelled at by mom or dad at home if we didn't do something right or forgot to do a chore or didn't somehow meet their expectations.

We likewise feared getting mocked by peers and siblings for our perceived flaws and imagined shortcomings. If we could not manage to do a simple task that, say, a sister or brother could do well, we felt like a failure. Again, fear stepped in as we, again, feared mockery, shunning, or worse.

My point is that we come very early to a relationship of sorts with fear. We come very early to our awareness of our flaws, our fears, and our failures—the "three Fs." In fact, as an adult, I see that we develop an over-awareness of them! They are like big red flashing lights that we can't tear our focus away from. We were never taught that, though these three Fs are all somewhat inherent to just being human, we can do something about them if we wish.

We were never taught how to turn them into something else or use them to our advantage. Now we can do that. We need first to embrace these attributes and not avoid them or go into denial about them. Don't shy away from them, but face them head on as personal challenges that we can and will overcome.

As I have gotten older, I look back at all the incredible things that I've accomplished: speaking in public, presenting in class or at work, writing books, marketing myself, achieving real sales. Yet, these were all the things that I had previously labeled as my flaws and failings. Weaknesses. Things that I feared doing the most.

I hated (well, feared really) speaking in public. I was never the best communicator throughout school. English was not my first language; my grammar was flawed. But by overcoming my fears, I actually started to face those challenges, to find a way to learn. I gritted my teeth and did the things I needed to do in order to turn those so-called flaws and failings into strengths. I turned my fears upside down and found that they transmuted into courage! More and more, I was doing what I thought I wasn't capable of.

Flaws Are Your Strength

Once I figured out that no matter who else I spent my life with, I was always going to be with Me... well, that tipped the scales and tilted me into that space of wanting to be the best Me I could become. This became a realization that bolstered me and strengthened my self-confidence.

This realization moved me to assessing my apparent flaws as something I no longer wanted to carry around, and from there, I identified what it was I wanted instead. What amazed me was that sometimes I didn't want to replace a flaw with anything at all! Its absence, its elimination, was enough for me.

I can give you an example of someone in the workplace who had people tearing their hair out because of her continuous interruptions during conversations, presentations, and business discussions. I had no interactions with her myself; however, of those who did have to deal with her, all tried hard to avoid engaging with her. Why? Because they would end up not getting a word in edgewise. They would end up not being allowed to complete any of their thoughts. They were sure she never heard a word they said. Her interrupting was definitely a flaw and a relationship buster, her coworkers thought.

Finally, her direct boss took action and sat with the person. The boss gave her straight, tough love and told her that she had to bring her compulsion to interrupt others under control or be booted off the team. Wow. Talk about a strong external motivator to make a change...

And so she did. She went to a personal coach her boss recommended. She followed the instructions the coach gave her. She did the practice that the coach expected of her. It didn't work overnight (remember three-month big, audacious goals and 30-60-90-day plans with their action items?). She asked for and received regular feedback from her boss and her most irritated coworkers over the weeks and months that followed.

When her coworkers realized she really was making an honest and sincere effort at transforming her old habit, they grew more supportive and willing to give her honest, not-judgmental feedback (remember soft goals and how one of your action items is to ask trusted people for progress reports or assessments?).

The coach revealed to her the source cause of her problem is the compulsion to interrupt, and from there the woman made a serious commitment to get to the end of it. At term, she made a shift in her behavior and became a most respected colleague that others knew would attentively listen. She came to a point of awareness that her coworkers had to occasionally prod her to speak up and contribute!

Moral of that story: *We have the personal power to make a change! By identifying some sabotaging flaw and accepting that it just is, we can take back our control over it. Turn it upside down. Turn it into a strength.*

I have found that by examining any of my flaws or weaknesses closely and dispassionately, I can pivot around it and see it from different perspectives. To achieve that, I cannot have strong judgments about it. I have to remind myself "it just is what it is right now."

It also helps to talk over your perspective with a trusted, supportive friend. You may discover that your friend has a very different viewpoint and description of what you call a flaw. Listen with an open mind, and you may discover that your flaw is quite a unique and welcomed character trait. But if (like the interrupter) your flaw is a saboteur, you also have tools to deal with it.

Anyone's biggest strength is self-awareness, followed (as our interrupter learned with his coach) by other-awareness. With awareness, you understand that there are areas of your life that are not your strongest. You can readily identify those areas that you should give more attention to. Awareness can be your biggest strength!

Fear Is Your Friend

Fear paralyzes us. It freezes our ability to think clearly. Fight or flight is a reaction to a danger, to a fright, to a fear. It is an old mechanism that today causes us chronic stress—a never-ending, constant stress—because we are all too often in fight or flight mode.

And yet, here I am, stating unequivocally that fear is your friend! Why?

Understand that our human brain is wired to guide you to do the things that are certain and known to you. We are wired for certainty and safety! That's why fear is such a big deal—it warns us that we have left, or will soon leave, our safe haven of certainty.

But you know what I learned? Fear is just a feeling. Just like joy, courage, or grief. We can process and let go of any feeling—any and all of them. All humans seem to have an overabundant supply of feelings, so if we just focus on one of them—fear—it is easier.

I was into self-improvement and success guru Tony Robbins' courses for a while, and he tells this story about two of his famous (but he wouldn't name them) private clients. They came to him separately. They were both famous singers with international fan bases. They both did a tremendous number of live performances.

What he noticed when working with them was that they had opposing reactions to what entertainers call stage fright. They both admitted to experiencing stage fright. They both knew it was just a feeling. However, the male performer succumbed to stage fright and let it become nearly debilitating. He'd break out in cold sweats, he would ring his hands, and he'd pace the floor backstage before coming out for his audience. In fact, he admitted to Tony that he was a wreck until the moment he grabbed the mic and spoke his first words to his fans. Then the stage fright would melt and he'd be in his star performance zone.

His second client was a female singer who acknowledged that stage fright existed for her, too. Contrary to the other client, she said it gave her energy; it pumped her up. She was ready for action. She felt like the world was at her feet and she could not only face the world but lead it where she wanted it to go. Talk about energized excitement!

And that is where the concept of courageousness comes in. Courage is the flipside of fear. These two singers demonstrate to us that we can choose which side of the coin wins and controls our emotional state. We can choose. We can decide. Do you choose fear? Or do you recognize it for what it is, flip the coin, and experience courage, excitement, and enthusiasm instead?

Were both of those famous singers successful? Yes and no. Which one had more success as far as self-awareness and self-control or emotional control? True success comes to those who see and recognize their fears and then overcome them by flipping that coin over to high-energy courage, excitement, passion, and enthusiasm.

Like the female vocalist, you can know to look at fears and use each and every one of them to your advantage. Go ahead right now and write down the first four answers that come to your mind to this question: "What are you afraid of?"

Then look at each response. Here is how that list of four fears might look for some people:

1. I'm afraid that I won't be able to deliver great results to my clients. (Fear of really being under-qualified; fear of looking like a fraud...)
2. I'm afraid of plowing all of my savings into this new business venture. (Fear of starting over financially; fear of failing...)

3. I'm afraid I am not good enough for my partner.
   (Fear of not being enough for him…)
4. I'm afraid I'm not being a good enough mother to
   my kids…

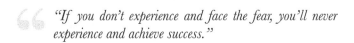

> *"If you don't experience and face the fear, you'll never experience and achieve success."*

Find the flip side of each of those coins and move from fear into courage, excitement, and enthusiasm instead. Here is how that could look for those fears I listed above…

1. This client decided to hire me after our consultation call. They understand that I'm great at this job. I have a great past track record. I *love* doing this kind of work! *I am who they need!*
2. I know all about this kind of business from many fruitful past experiences. I am a successful, highly-driven person, and I can make a go of this *and* earn my savings back. And more!
3. My partner knows what I am. I am *enough. I am whole and complete just as I am.*
4. I know I will do my best to take care of my kids;, my best will be good enough!

Failure Is Your Teacher

Failure is only a negative if we choose to see it in that light. We saw in the preceding chapter how a failure can be seen as a terrific success. The sales team was sure they had failed to meet their annual sales goal of $15M. Well, they were right, because they did not bring in $15M. But was that really a failure? The salespeople themselves saw it as a team failure. But was it a failure for the business? Apparently not. It was the bosses who saw the $13.5M in sales as a success, because it was $3.5 million more than they had earned the prior year!

In that scenario, the bosses were the ones who flipped the coin to demonstrate to their team how an apparent failure easily becomes a success. It's about perception. As they say in politics, perception is the reality. But I am telling you… you get to choose the perception you hold in mind.

You are the only one who can make a failure feel like a negative. Which one of these statements feels better to you?

1. We failed to reach our $15M sales goal.
2. We brought in $3.5M more for the business this year than last year.

I would much rather repeat to myself the second statement than the first.

It is only a failure until you reposition your viewpoint, so… pivot! It is only a failure if it has kept you from moving forward and trying again. Repositioning is about shifting your thinking into a new direction. Marketing people reposition products and advertising messages all the time in order to more clearly communicate to customers what they have to offer.

What happened with the sales team is that they sat together to reposition their thinking. They sat together to reconfirm as a unit that they were willing and able to move forward and try again for the $15M. They examined their sales approaches, their sales philosophies, their sales tools. They also examined whether they were making excuses for themselves as individuals or as a team, or if there were real reasons blocking their attainment of the big, audacious goal. In other words, they used their so-called failure as an opportunity. They reevaluated. They readjusted. They reenergized (their leadership's positive reaction really helped) and came back stronger than ever.

One of the salespeople even concluded something quite philosophical: *failure to reach a goal is not fatal.* Failure to reach a goal still allows for success. Failure simply means that you get another chance to **hit the jackpot.**

Failure is an amazing teacher. When I was learning about operating a business, I heard a business consultant at a meetup speak about a client of hers who was a "startup junkie." With her assistance, the client had devised two interesting business concepts, discussed strategy, and written up both business plans. He carried out the soft launch and moved into the hard launch of each one, and the businesses both failed to catch on. He closed operations immediately. He told the consultant that doing this two times was worth more than a Harvard MBA!

What he was really saying is that *without failure we don't learn.* Change your thinking about failure. Don't see it as a crushing blow to your success, but as information you can analyze about the path you chose and the approach you used.

Remember goal to effort? Just because we failed to hit a goal doesn't mean we didn't gain anything in return. There's always a great lesson that can be learned from any failure. As long as you put in your best efforts, that's all you need.

Change Your Mind(set)

What I have been talking about here is mindset. Although it might sometimes be upsetting to realize you have not reached your big, audacious goal, with a slight pivot and a change of perspective, you can identify the real success you have achieved and all the lessons you have learned:

- You achieved two out of three of your goals? Celebrate the gain.

- You now know how to approach your next soft goal for better results? Celebrate the learning!
- Failure in a relationship is a great way to understand what makes people tick. Celebrate the new insights.
- Failure of your startup business? It is a great opportunity to ask yourself if you were too rigid in your approach and whether you needed to pivot!

Flaws? Fears? Failures? All it takes is a slight change in perspective so you can leverage them to propel you forward. Change your view of those "three Fs" by looking at them from the flip side of each coin. One side of that coin is going to be the yin, the other side the yang. Get a balanced perspective by flipping and examining both sides of the coin. Celebrate the fact that all this learning you have been doing is maker you wiser, more self-aware, more other-aware, more balanced.

No matter what you do in life, you are bound to encounter the 3 Fs sometimes. Use them to your advantage. See them not as your enemy but instead as partners who propel you forward to your goals. Like strength training and lifting weights, the dumbbell doesn't get lighter, but YOU get stronger in the process.

10

YOUR PROBLEM IS NOT WHAT YOU THINK

W e've just seen that those three Fs of fear, flaws, and failure are not really the problems you thought they were. Likewise, your problem isn't procrastination, laziness, or lack of motivation.

What is it then, since we are all convinced there must be a problem? Your problem is discipline.

Some people lack the discipline to follow through with any of their goals, like those infamous New Year's resolution goals. There is a problem, but it originates in *how* you have set the goal in the first place. You've seen how to line up values and purpose behind a goal, and how to map out your 30-60-90-day plan to reach it. That definitely helps to have that follow-through.

Do you remember Nike's famous "Just Do It" campaign? Just doing it—no matter what, no matter the weather, no matter the obstacles, no matter the pain—is what discipline is all about.

We should look at purpose as the foundation for discipline. You have seen that you use purpose and values to help you identify whether or not the goals you are setting are the right ones for you. If you start out your journey with no purpose and no values, then soon, something will go wrong. No amount of discipline will propel you meaningfully to the goal.

Discipline is a powerful driver when it comes to achieving big goals and dreams. However, discipline must operate hand in hand with your purpose—to get you going, to keep you going, and lead you all the way to the finish line. When you know "the goal behind your goal," discipline is right there to support you.

A feeling of excitement on its own will not work to carry you to your big, audacious goal achievement. Think of excitement for your goal as the honeymoon that precedes years of living together. As the saying goes, the honeymoon is soon over. When the blush fades from your goal, you call on your self-discipline to propel you forward. The values that you have put underneath your goal will put the blush back in you, and momentum and discipline will come more easily.

The best way to start any big, audacious venture is by taking small steps, completing small actions, and repeating the process daily. That is our goal-setting map. Remember, that is what we have done, as we have chunked down each of our hard and soft goals into goal plans of 30-60-90 days' duration. We have chunked down the plan into actionable items that you will need to take in order to hit those goals. Those action items will act as your daily reminders, representing your small steps that you need to take and repeat daily with determination until you have achieved the big goal.

Those small daily actions train your discipline level in a way similar to how you train your body. Taking those daily steps is comparable to physical strength training—no future bodybuilder starts by lifting 375 pounds, but starts at smaller weights and works her way to the heaviest ones. The smaller weights for the lifter are equivalent of our small action steps to achieve each mini-goal. As we complete each action item and complete each mini-goal (increase the weight we practice lifting), we become more confident and more disciplined.

Like the bodybuilder, the harder you train your discipline muscle—by using the incremental steps called values, purpose, goal, and your 30-60-90-day plans—the more practiced you will become in achieving any of your hard or soft goals.

Discipline is a key component in achieving goals. Discipline is a muscle. Discipline, supported by setting your yin-yang goals the right way, is your goal-getting friend!

How to Sustain Your Level of Discipline

The way to strengthen your discipline muscle (and this sounds silly, I know) is a version of the Nike motto: just use it. One of your discipline-strengthening and sustaining tools is your daily action item structure.

Ambitious women are busy women. If you're like me, you know individuals who can get up any time of the morning or afternoon they wish, go to bed at any time they feel like it, and their life rolls along just fine. I don't function like that and you probably don't either… ambitious women just don't.

By giving a structure to my day, disciplining myself to stick to my goal-producing action list is much easier. Sure, we could all float along with our To Do list in our heads. But that is not really structured. By knowing *in writing* (you have seen that I love to write!) what activities I will be performing throughout the day, planning what part of the day I must do these activities is the structure that works for me.

I once knew an overweight guy in college. One day he decided enough was enough. He put an alarm in his phone for exactly the time he would be arriving home from his daily classes and evening job. That alarm meant: *"Put on your running shoes; they are in your trunk so no need to go up to your apartment—and GET WALKING!"* College students are sort of geeky about using their smartphones, and that single alarm prodded him to do his one-hour walk before he even went up to his apartment. Because he was so big, and one hour of walking was sweaty work, his next move was a long shower and fresh clothes. Then his evening could begin. That discipline paid off. He lost 80 pounds that school year. The only thing that really did it for him was the repetitive, disciplined "just do it" after work each night. He likes to say that if he ever had gone up to his apartment on any given evening, he would never have gone back out for the walk.

This is where values and purpose come back into the picture to support you. If your goal is aligned with a heartfelt core value, and if your goal is backed by a strong, important, beneficial purpose for you, all you need is that structure and a determined mental decision to just do it. Like the overweight walker, part of your structure is having an action item to do each and every day. If, like the overweight walker, you perform your action for that goal at the same time every day, that habit formation strengthens the structure and your discipline to perform the action. By doing things like the walker did, you lessen the mental resistance to just doing it. You make it more effortless to just do it; in effect, you automate things for yourself. You don't have to think about it, because if you are on automatic and its 8:00 p.m., you automatically shoe up and just do it.

Motivational success speaker Mel Robbins calls her just-do-it trick the "5 second rule." When your smartphone alarm tells you it's 8:00 p.m, you immediately start counting backwards from five and by the time you hit one, you must already be doing the action item on your To Do list. Wait any longer and your mind will start giving you all sorts of reasons you should not be doing this but something else.

Get Your Subconscious on Board

When people talk about mental blocks, or about how they start listening to their negative self-talk or how their mind got in the way, it is the subconscious they are referring to. The subconscious has a job, and that job is to block you from doing anything different from your normal routine. If it starts to kick in, take your subconscious on a trip into the future. Take it to a time when your goal is already attained. Give your subconscious a sensorial review how your life looks, sounds, and feels because that goal has been achieved.

The subconscious operates from the senses (seeing, feeling, hearing, touching, smelling). Here is how that sensorial review might look:

1. *See* your goal achieved—visualize how that looks. See a mental picture. If you are not a visual person, paint that picture for your subconscious with colorful, descriptive words in your head.
2. *Feel* the new feeling(s) you feel when you have done the thing, such as excitement, pride, exuberant joy, quiet knowingness, etc. It is important to reproduce that feeling in your body, even briefly.
3. *Hear* what you say and what others say about you upon that success: "She really did it AND we knew she had it in her!" etc.

That is how to get the subconscious on board with your goal. That is how to keep the subconscious from blocking your disciplined actions. This sensorial self-talk pulls you back on track and into a state of self-discipline again.

To reiterate, some strategies that help you build strong self-discipline include:

- Reflect on your core values, what they mean to you deeply and how it makes you feel
- Always reminding yourself, on a daily basis, what your why and purpose is behind the big, audacious goal.
- Chunking your goals into 30-60-90-day periods, ensuring that you are taking steps to do those action items that were written up in your goal-setting map.

The Boring Stuff (aka Consistency) Turns Dreams into a Reality

A Japanese proverb is "Nana korobi, ya oki," which means, "Fall down seven times, stand up eight."

It is perfectly fine to set lofty hard or soft goals for anything you want and line them up with your values and purpose. We are going to fall or stumble a step or two. That is part of reaching high. But we can't achieve anything sprawled on the sidewalk! That is where grit and determination come in. That is where brushing yourself off and moving along come in.

Discipline isn't about always staying upright and moving down the road. Discipline is the ability to fall down—with grace!—but also to accept a helping hand to get back on your feet when you cannot pick yourself back up. Then, just get back to running. That is the heart of grit and discipline: Fall seven times, get up eight.

Seek to be your best self by practicing consistency, persistence, and tenacity. Ambitious women don't give up. They just do it, exercising their discipline muscle frequently and regularly.

The more consistent you are in setting goals in alignment with your values and with a strong purpose and benefit to you, the more passionate you will be to attain those goals.

I have a girlfriend who had some health problems—quite scary ones at such a young age. The doctor examined, tested, and questioned her. Then this wise doctor told her all the problems—her entire diagnosis and all its symptoms—could be 100 percent resolved through a different set of food choices. The doctor told her exactly what foods to eat; the rest were absolutely and forever off the table. He used tough love and likewise made it quite clear that she would suffer lifelong from these afflictions if she did not make the dietary changes. Wow...

At the heart of it all, it sounds easy enough, right? My girl-friend 1) got the correct diagnosis, 2) was given the perfect heal-all-forever solution, and 3) received a clear structure (eat this, not that). Yet (you guessed it), she struggled.

Changing our food habits is one of the hardest things we do. Unless you have grown up with a physician schooled in nutrition or a trained nutritionist, most of us don't learn as children what the healthy foods to eat really are. We eat what our parents serve us, for the most part at least. As adults making our own choices, we fall back on what/how we ate as kids. We spend zero time in reflection on whether it's healthy or not.

That was my girlfriend's dilemma too. She trusted her physician 100 percent. She discovered, however, that she did not trust herself to muster up the discipline and just make the change. It was much too radical of a difference from her usual diet.

We chatted. I told her I was writing this book. I told her about big, audacious goals, and she admitted she frankly had one with this dietary switch! Then I told her she didn't need to make the change overnight or go cold turkey. We talked about values, purpose, chunking the end goal down into a 30-60-90-day plan, action items to follow through on a daily/weekly basis—the whole process you've just read. She thought that could work for her. I played the part of her coach to help her formulate her values and the big, audacious goal. She did see how her values lined up with the health and diet goal.

We discussed back and forth what kind of changes she could easily make within a 30-day timeframe and how she could be sure to stick with the change she made for years to come. We debated back and forth what would be the actionable items she would need to take to complete the switch into the new diet. I let her decide for herself and she came up with four action items to do over the coming month.

I got a call in week two; my friend was in tears. She had fallen off the wagon, so to speak, and was beating herself up about it. I told her the Japanese proverb. She got it. The next day she was back on track. All she needed was just another voice telling her she can do it, and I tried my best to be there for here, every moment of it!

Long story short, in the first month, she called me about seven times either in tears or ranting and raging about how she "could not do this anymore." Each time I reminded her of her heartfelt core value and purpose and the benefits she would gain from achieving this big, audacious health-restoring goal. I reminded her what she had told me about the core value she aligned with this goal, and how no one ever backs off from their core values. I told her what discipline really is: doing what you don't want to do but must, and not doing what you want to do because it is counter to your goals.

She followed through for a whole year with this plan! At the three-month point and then at the one-year mark, her doctor saw her. At three months, the doctor told her that her labs and markers were improving. That was a total high for my girlfriend and she did more than one Happy Dance! At one year, she was fully in the "normal" ranges. Yet, her doctor helped my friend and me out by stating that it wasn't a "once and done" pill that she had just taken. It was a lifetime habit that she needed to continuously commit to in order to maintain her restored health.

Moral of that story: *Never, ever give up. When you fall, get back up, have a cup of hot tea (no sugar, not on the "allowed" list!), and get back to your goal! Use the support that is all around you. Follow your goal-setting map. You can and will always make it, but only if you believe that yourself.*

11

LEARN TO EMBRACE CHANGE

L ife is nothing but continuous change. Just when you think you have got yourself into the all-time perfect zone, bam! Something happens that turns it upside down.

In more ways than one, we need to be nimble, flexible, and willing to turn on a dime. This goes for our jobs and livelihoods, our relationships, our health—and it goes for our goals as well.

In these pages, I have helped you set and take action to attain fairly short-term hard and soft goals. But do you really know what's going to happen between today and six months from now? None of us do. We can better imagine what's going to happen in 15 days, but that is not a given either.

Part of life is knowing that you will occasionally have to pivot and stretch to catch the curve ball that life pitched your way, just out of your reach. You might do a face-plant to catch it, but remember the Japanese saying about falling down and getting up.

The inevitability of change is why it is okay to set aside your current goals in favor of different, new ones that better address your changed circumstances. When you start to feel that the current goal you have set for yourself is not fitting anymore, please don't hold on to it! Drop it like a hot potato and move on. You might feel that you are taking two steps forward and one step back, but being adaptable in this way is far better than quitting altogether.

As I write these words, the nation I live in is still in the thick of the COVID-19 shutdowns and quarantines. Most school-aged kids are not back in the classroom. Travel, both domestic and international, is possible but challenging. Entrepreneurs have either seen their entire business flushed down the toilet, or have innovatively scrambled to adapt to social distancing pressures and saved some part of their revenues. Ordering anything online for delivery now demands that we forego that former "instant gratification" expectation. People are anxious about the real risk of getting evicted from their apartments, or having their home or condo foreclosed on. Face masks are the new fashion state-ment and are required in "public places." Lots of us are working remotely (i.e., from our homes) and still haven't figured out how to balance the kids' needs, work time, sanity, and… fill in the blank. Talk about change in one's life!

The year 2020 has indeed been rich in changes and chal-lenges of all kinds. On New Year's Day 2020, almost none of us on the planet had a clue that society and life in the work-place as we knew it would be suspended. People have had to do just what we're speaking of: turn on a dime, let go of New Year's resolutions, and older goals and routines. We've set our sights in a different direction by necessity. We are moving forward without really being sure where we'll end up in a month, in three, in six.

Even though we've all been in our homes a great deal this year, it is not at all certain that we have regained the equilib-rium lost in the first few crazy weeks of the pandemic responses. And balance is important—we mustn't neglect one aspect of our life for very long in favor of another. Yet, maybe that is what we are doing.

Balance is vital. I believe it's about making deposits into and withdrawals from our "emotional and mental bank accounts." Here's how that might look...

You had a crazy, intense workload for 14 hours two days in a row. You've been online so long you forget what blue skies and sunshine look like. Those two days of single-focus attention have depleted your emotional and mental bank accounts. By that I mean you had to make a "withdrawal" of extra attention span, extra stamina, extra self-control in order to stay the course and do your work. And it drained you somewhat.

Your work is done, so you pivot and make a change. You spend some time doing yoga with your three-year-old son, who hilariously pretends he can do some of the postures (and he can... sort of), all the while jabbering merrily to you. He finally has mom's attention and you zoom in on how he is, what he's communicating, and on his exuberant energy. You make a "deposit" into your emotional and mental accounts, this time of renewed energy and uplifting joy. You have more energy now, more happiness, and you've emptied your mind of work worries. All is well (or better) in your world.

When was the last time you did yoga in the living room on a Tuesday at 2:20 p.m. with your child? Never! So when change hits, look for the benefits and gains as well. Making that deposit into your account rebuilds your emergency reserves and will help you through down times or insane high-pressure work days.

It's okay to have single-focus days, bad days, and even unproductive days! Not every day will qualify as your best day, so just go with it. The up-and-down cyclical movement of your days ends up in balance.

I know friends who have "skip" days, mental health days, or spa days. What they are all doing in their own way is taking leave of absence. They are switching gears. They are resetting the clock. Getting back into harmony internally. They are making deposits in the account.

Those skip days could be the one day each week you just don't have to follow your weight loss diet or do that five-mile run. That spa day might be a couple's day, a getaway with your husband to take a break from the house, the jobs, the kids, the smartphones. It reconnects you and brings things back into a happier perspective.

My skip day is when I just stay away from my business and my smartphone and "veg out." Yes, sometimes that's hard when I feel so driven by purpose, the clock, and the To Do list. But the next day I have never regretted having that down time.

These are all alternative ways to make a deposit in your emotional and mental bank accounts and to build up an "emergency" reserve of sorts.

What Balance Really Means

Most people have the wrong understanding of "balance." It's not always about a 50/50 balance between our time and our efforts. Getting to a 50/50 stance is not actually the intention.

Balance—that yin-yang of our lives—is more about knowing yourself, understanding or having a deep awareness of when it is time to make a deposit in your emotional/mental bank. Whether you just finished a soft launch of your new business, or finished a hard project at your job, you know that those were times when you were definitely not living a 50/50 balance! Sometimes, we drive hard at one aspect of life because that is what we have to do at that time. *The key is understand that it won't, or shouldn't, be what we do forever.* We will soon step back into a yin-yang balance.

Be Flexible Enough to Change – Even Your Goals

If COVID quarantining and business shutdowns have taught us nothing else, it is how flexible and adaptable we are—or refuse to be. Some of us just can't pivot, I get that. But to get the goals you set for yourself, you'll nonetheless need to be nimble, allow for change, and be flexible.

While goals can help you get where you want to be, some-times those sudden changes in your life throw a wrench in the works. You let go of the goal—or it has had to let go of you. It is alright! It is not "do or die." You might feel you are backtracking 10x, but your attention and energy is clearly needed elsewhere for the time being.

So, stay loose. Don't be "married" to that goal when change hits you between the eyes and demands that you pivot. Allow yourself to pivot away from the past goal and over to the issues and needs now at hand. Stay in balance.

Stay loose when it comes to goal setting. Allow yourself the flexibility to let it go (or to let it go until some future time) and get clarity about your new situation. Chances are you'll find a goal that resonates better or empowers you even more.

When changes occur in your life, it is not just your goals that leave you, but your initial core values and purpose (your why) might shift as well:

- You got married and/or became pregnant, and that meant (it doesn't always, but it did for you) that your core values changed: "family first and investing in kids" is your brand-new top core value… and your new purpose.

- You got laid off recently, and serendipitously discovered a new interest in another career and in a different industry; you have new purpose, which means your former career and professional goals must be revisited, too.
- You got a diagnosis, a health ultimatum of sorts like my friend, and now you need to do things that you have never done before or even considered! You may put current goals on the shelf for now (because nothing supersedes ensuring good health) and set new goals that help you change old habits, commit to new ones, and track your return to health.

Life happens and, before your very eyes, things pivot. A need for personal change hits you smack between the eyes. Things can change drastically in your world in the bat of an eye. Act on what your eyes are seeing! Set different goals.

Other Signs That It Is Time to Change Goals

Sometimes nothing really extraordinary has happened in your world to trigger a change of goals. And still, something is off. Ask yourself about the goals you are working on in light of the following considerations:

- You realize you are working someone else's goal(s), doing it to meet someone else's expectations of you.
- You have accepted someone else's purpose and set goals based on them rather than on purposes that deeply resonate with you.
- One or more of your goals is fear-driven instead of purpose-driven.
- You are focused on only one aspect of life, even

when you have multiple goals, and feel the
unhappiness of that imbalance.

Are you working on your partner's goal instead of something
for you? Are you working on society's expectations of you? A
good way to test for that is to go back to the core value and
purpose behind each of your goals. If it is your husband's
core value but not yours, change goals. If it is society's reason
but not yours, change goals. Change, so you have that
alignment.

Society's expectations will run against the grain for many
people. But you hate to color outside the lines, to take a
detour off the well-beaten path. Because of that, you set
goals out of fear of being singled out from the crowd rather
than from passion and purpose of your own.

Feverishly trying to achieve someone else's goals or having
unrealistic expectations of your own "progress" in life create
imbalances that get us grumpy. Dedicating all your waking
hours to just one aspect of your life or to just one type of
goal (only body goals, only money goals, etc.) will only cause
you to feel miserable most of the time. You are a
multifaceted human and it is natural to give a portion of
your attention to the different aspects of who you are and
what you love.

One of my dear friends gave birth to a baby girl earlier this
year. Motherhood is truly an amazing journey for her and
she is not your typical stay-at-home mom (is there such a
thing?). While she is an amazing wife to her husband, she's
also her own boss leading a team of over 10 in her consulting
business. She's hardworking, passionate, and incredibly kind.

But life pivoted for her after she became a mother. Her priorities shifted due to her newborn; she called me for advice
because she wanted help. She felt like she was at a point

where there were just too many things to do and not enough time in the day.

You can guess what I told her. I advised her to start setting goals for herself. She looked at me and said, "Selina, no way! Seriously? We're adults now, we don't need goals! … Uhhh… Do we?"

I told her, "Yes way! Seriously! It's the only way to learn to balance the different roles you have now. If you don't want to feel stuck, the only way forward is to set meaningful hard and soft goals for yourself. Do it for the sake of your family… and your sanity."

My mention of "soft goals" got her roped in. We went through the goal-getting map. Her biggest priorities (which she called her values) were 1) **motherhood** – raising her daughter, 2) **love** – harmony in her immediate and extended family, and 3) **success** for her business. She set up distinctive goals and identified her why for each of those values.

She clearly understands that this year it will be hard for her to put 100 percent on her consulting work, but her daughter comes first, and she is seeing the bigger picture due to setting the proper goals that align with her own current needs, her values, and her why. She knows she cannot do it all (at least this year), but now she has direction and focus.

We catch up at least once a month, and she tells me how much happier she is. She no longer feels like she's out of time, low on energy, or grumpy all day. She feels at peace and can take everything in stride (almost) stress-free!

Though I'm not a mother but want to be in coming years, I've seen so many of my friends and colleagues go through this dilemma, struggling to toggle between their kids and their business/work. The real precious key here is to remember that your kids will only be young once; they won't be babies forever. But (and this is what we forget) your business/success/career will always be there. Sometimes it is okay to not be a superwoman and try to be the best in all these areas of our lives. We have to learn to pivot and adapt to changes or else we will end up getting lost in our purpose and lose motivation to go about our days.

Remember, you can always bring yin-yang into your life. Everything might not feel like 50/50 for you *right now,* but eventually it will all come to a greater balance—that is the life we are all striving for.

No one—literally none of us—has it all perfect. We all have to learn to be flexible, adapt to fires, and be ready to take on whatever it is that life throws at us, but what stands out among the strong, ambitious women from the rest is we're able to tip the scale back when that storm is over.

The Balance Wheel

There is another way of interpreting the concept of balance.

Plot your core values in this presentation of a balance wheel, I've used my own example for reference here:

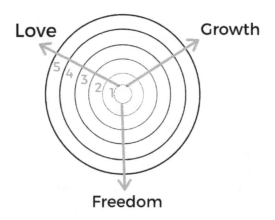

This is called a wheel for a good reason.

Before you get started, your balance wheel is probably off balance now, one core value might be weighing significantly heavier than the others, but that's okay, that's exactly why we set goals in the first place. Once you've gone through the entire 90 days period, you will gradually tip the scale back to an even, equilibrium state.

Remember that I said earlier how achieving one goal can affect a completely different part of your life? That is because of the synergy of our efforts and the synergy of our multifaceted beings. If you consciously aim to have a handful of goals in different areas of your life, first you balance things out, and then the synergy of working on two or three very different goals boosts the effects in other areas of your life you're working on. Because the goals that you've set for yourself will resonate with your own core values, this will help keep your balance wheel at an equilibrium or even state.

I have talked to people working on their medical health or body fitness, and heard them exclaim what a beneficial impact it seemed to have on their work life or their relationships at home. Just as we are today connected to everyone in the world through the Internet of Things in our digital technologies, every area we work to improve will improve other areas of our lives as well.

It's all connected! Nature tends towards a gentle equilibrium of your yin-yang. You help it along with your soft and hard goals work when pivoting and changing your goals in times of change might be a necessity. But having a range of goals across areas of your life might be refreshing and re-energizing most of the time!

Yin-yang and balance will indeed sometimes call for you to be flexible. To turn on a dime. To toss out a goal in midstream for another one that is more relevant or urgent in this moment. Be willing to shelve a goal (for now), to change and adapt by setting new ones. Not just individuals but sometimes a whole society needs to test its own equilibrium and swing hard in one direction or another before settling back into a new, more appropriate balance.

12

STOP SETTLING FOR LESS

There are so many benefits to setting goals, and I hope you see that now. Contrarily, there are downsides of not setting goals at all. The major one in my mind is that you just float along, letting life happen to you. I would frankly rather take control of my life by setting and getting goals. I am much more certain of creating the life I want when I aim for a specific set of goals.

A friend of mine who is somewhat older than I am was earning a juicy mid-six-figure income straight out of college. Sure, she was doing the work she had been trained to do in college. Not everyone can say that. But she was all about the work. That was her primary focus, and indeed it was her whole life. She felt like a great success because she was doing the work she had trained for and earned a degree to perform. But she admitted to me that a few years into this single-focus life, she was feeling burnt out. She was feeling like she was fading away or becoming invisible in the world. She said it was a very, very spooky feeling indeed. It was as though, she said, she had no existence outside of her job. She didn't have an intimate or romantic relationship. Not on her radar. She didn't do anything in particular with her piles of money—no investments, no interest-paying savings account, but also no spending sprees online or in shops, either for her residence or her person. Again, not on her radar.

She kept coming back to me looking older than her years, listless and lifeless, uninterested in most topics of conversation. She finally blurted out to me one day, "Selina, how is it you look so energized every day and seem to do so much more with your life than I can manage?"

And so we talked about setting goals. About values. About not just setting any frivolous goal, but goals that have a definite purpose underlying and supporting them. Daring to think big, and to set big goals—but then to chunk them down into bite-sized doable tasks. Especially, though, knowing her tendency have only a single focus in life, I talked about the Balance Wheel and the multifaceted person she really is without acknowledging it.

I don't know what exactly triggered her, but that fired her up then and there (it certainly had been ages since I saw her like that...). She got out a digital tablet and started firing questions to me and typing what I responded.

We didn't see each other for nearly five weeks after that. But when we did, I almost did not recognize her! She was vibrant. Her eyes sparkled. I swear that even her posture had corrected itself and her complexion was different.

Then I realized what had happened: She was happy! She babbled on and on (unlike the friend I had talked to barely a month earlier!) about her goals. Amazingly, and happily, none of those goals had anything to do with her career! She was working on making herself "more well-rounded." She was in control not just of her job and career now, but also of her entire life. She found a new hobby of knitting and started going on more dates to hopefully one day meet her signifi-cant other. She finally felt like herself and started to live a life that she was happy about.

Five Major Downsides of NOT Setting Goals

The moral of that story: There are major, major downsides to not setting goals. Have a look at the list below, and then have a look at your own lopsided Balance Wheel.

You will recognize a couple of downsides from my girl-friend's story. How many of them apply to you? Here are five more disadvantages to not setting (and working toward getting) some soft and hard goals:

1. **People Pleasing**: You will end up living in everyone else's version of what they want you to be rather than your own.

Goals help us tap into our inner strengths and develop them to be even stronger. Every little success, every mini-goal achieved, or any small action item performed on a date that you really didn't want to do it, it all increases your sense of confidence and self-worth and confirms that you have poten-tial for more.

When you people-please, you are developing what other people would like to be your strengths. What that means is they want you to improve your weaknesses instead of focusing on what you do well.

This goes back to setting the wrong goals because you are trying to fulfill others' expectations of you and ignoring your own passions and desires. It will not end well!

It's okay to say NO, and goals will help you do that. By knowing what your goals are, you can confidently say no to things that won't help you progress.

2. **Lack of Control**: You are no longer in control of your future… nor, really, of your present.

If you don't set goals for yourself that are purposeful and passionate for you, you will forever be trying to achieve other people's goals for you. You may love these individuals and they may be very well intentioned. However, they want to live through you which prevents you from living on your own as a result of making your own choices and decisions. They may be control freaks and not let you live your life at all. In short, they are controlling your life... and you are letting them do it. You have given up your personal power.

Life just happens to you and you go through life without a rudder, aka all those heartfelt personal goals that you have chosen. Life is unfulfilling when you are trying to reach other people's imposed goals.

Take your personal power back! If you do a daily action item, even a small one towards reaching your mini-goal and then your big, audacious goal, you are molding your future as you want it to be.

If you know exactly what you want your future to look like, but you're not applying the steps of our goal-setting map, then you can't blame anyone else but yourself.

Identify your values. Identify what it is you no longer want to have in your life. Turn that upside down and make it into a goal for something you do passionately want instead. See your own purpose behind that goal (the goal behind the goal). Break it down into any number of mini-goals. Assign action items to each mini-goal... and get going!

3. **Wasted Time**: Years will go by before you realize you never started your passion business, you never made that investment, you never did that overseas travel, you never

settled down and had those two kids you dreamed about as an older teen, etc. Will it be too late?

Talking about control that you have over your life, how are you spending your time? I know it is cliché, but we all have the same 24 hours per day allotted to us. It is not so much the time but what you are doing with it that counts.

You don't have to be productive every single minute of your day. In fact, that might even be counterproductive. But you do need to have some activities (soft and hard goals work) that build toward a different desired future for you.

If you sleep seven hours a night, and spend 13 hours at work (including the commute to and from your workplace), you still have four free hours to create your life through goal setting and goal getting. Or are you spending it cruising Instagram or YouTube? I'd frankly prefer to finish my daily action item (that will help me reach my goals), and then leave the extra time to do whatever I want.

Outside of work (and even while working, quite often) you are in control of how you spend your time. Control yourself and your time. Period.

4. **Focus**: Either you have no focus or clear direction at all, or you focus your entire attention and energy on only one aspect of your life (career, business) and eventually suffer from the imbalance you yourself created.

In this 21st century (as said by my parents and other elders), we are bombarded with digital distractions. How sharp a focus can you keep on something that doesn't interest you or on something that exhausts you?

Set goals that align with your core values and provide you with a strong purpose or why. Set your own goals, those that move you toward a more desirable future state that you have envisioned. When it is your goal, your new future, your strong core value, and your heartfelt purpose, you easily remain focused, sharp, and attentive to your goal-setting map. Have multiple goals addressing different areas of your life, and you will have balance that energizes you. The variety pulls you in and motivates you to go all the way to your big, audacious goal achievement.

Being able to focus on something you are passionate about gives you a clear direction on what exactly you need to spend your time and energy on. It helps you filter out the 1,002,032 other things in your life that your mind tells you to worry about. Goals create a mental filter for you so that your focus can be better allocated to things that matter to you and your personal growth.

5. **No Growth Mindset**: "In this world you're either growing or you're dying, so get in motion and grow." (Lou Holtz)

Any one of us who has been in the workforce for over six months knows this: If you're not improving, you get passed over. No bonus, no promotion, no offer of training. And soon? No job! Why wouldn't it be the same in life?

Life on Earth is both challenging and fascinating because of the humans on the planet! If everybody were the same, this world would be a dull and dreary place to live in. I would like to think that my friends, my partner, my colleagues, and people I haven't even met yet will find me to be interesting, a woman of eclectic interests, talents, and skills. Mind you, I am not seeking elected office! But when I find other people interesting and express my interest in them, I know they open up much more comfortably and quickly. I am just turning the tables and making myself that interesting person that they connect with quickly.

People will sense your high, light, and vibrant energy when you are on a path of personal growth. People will be magnetically drawn to you, and that won't be a bad thing for harmonious relationships, learning new things, being offered new jobs, and so much more. Don't miss out. Set and get goals.

ALMOST THERE...

I'm assuming if you've read all way close to the end, that means

1) You loved the book so much that you couldn't wait to finish it!

2) You loved the book so much that you were expecting more?!

Just kidding :) or maybe I'm right.

Either way, I'm sure you wouldn't have made it to this page, if you didn't truly resonate with everything I've talked about in the book.

Now I just want to ask you for one tiny favor.

If you enjoyed my book, it would mean the world to me if you can leave your feedback in the review section.

A sentences or two, a paragraph, doesn't matter: just tell me how you really feel after everything you've learned here, I want to hear it all.

Please scan the QR code below to leave your review:

Thank you again from the bottom of my heart!

Though, you're not quite done here, remember the *"You Can Have It All"* chapter I mentioned in the beginning of this book? That's what the next (and last) few pages is all about, and I'm sure you're going to love it, now just read on, because you're sooo close to the finish line.

YOU CAN HAVE IT ALL

I ask you, the ambitious woman, to look now at your soft and hard goals as a means to an end, not the end itself.

Goal setting and goal getting is not about validating yourself as a superwoman; that is not the goal at all. The purpose is to use this framework of Goal-Setting to allow you to gain more control, to ease the stress, and most importantly, to help you cultivate your best life. You can be an ambitious woman, successful boss, and also the amazing girlfriend, wife, or mother. You can have it all. Don't let anyone else tell you other wise.

The ultimate goal behind the ensemble of your goals is to create a continuous yin-yang balance in your life overall. To feel in control and happy of the life you are living. To have a process to change anything that is not working for you, and know that you can do it without debilitating stress. To have a way to turn on a dime when a massive shift occurs in your life.

What we are all seeking as we pursue a combination of soft and hard goals throughout our lives is balance, a sense of personal control, a sense of effortlessness. We don't just focus

—like businesses do—only on hard measurable goals that must be met (or else!). Remember that the balance of yin-yang means that we pursue soft goals alongside hard ones. We pursue personal internal well-being and growth goals alongside outer, material-world goals.

You can have it all, and building that "all" is an evolving balancing act that unfolds over the years of our lives. Soft and hard goals keep you in equilibrium.

You may have long stretches of time when everything seems to have lined up perfectly for you. We love those times! Or you may have those times where nothing in your life feels like it's going forward—your life is so far off balance. That's when you need to kick back into your yin-yang way, become a goal-setter, and goal-getter to turn your life around.

You can be your own "agent of change," and within a short period of time, you can dramatically change the path you have been on. You can surround yourself with very different people. You can create a new living and working environment. You can experience a higher level of abundance and happiness for yourself.

All that takes is a purposeful decision, the right kind of process to stay on track, and an awareness of the yin-yang balance among all the areas of your life. Balance is what makes you happy and keeps you healthy while you grow into yourself.

With my soft goals approach in combination with some hard goals, you create balance and harmony. You become more of who you can be. You create more balance and happiness with yourself and your life.

The Journey

Beware, though, of the arrival fallacy: We never _are_ the master. We are only _becoming_ a master. Becoming is a lifelong evolution, not a final destination where we rest on our laurels.

Just because you've achieved your goals doesn't mean that you have arrived at any kind of definitive mastership, or at any kind of end destination where you stop for good and settle in. Sure, life is full of stopovers and stop-offs. It is full of places to pause and reflect, to smell the roses and enjoy the view. But none of those places is your end goal.

While some might say that the ultimate goal in our lives is to be imperturbably happy and to experience unconditional love, you might ask me, "Why don't we start there instead of going for all these material goals?" And I would respond, "Yes, indeed, why not start there?" That is why early in these pages I talked about putting your happiness first!

And then when you've created your happiness and are beginning to experience the vastness of love, you can go out and create other goals that help you create the worldly life you choose, alongside the inner being person that you are *becoming*.

Goals represent an ongoing process for achieving that new inner being state, that new outer life, that enhanced happiness, that more widely experienced and shared love. And they represent ways of creating the yin/yang balanced, fulfilling life we have chosen for ourselves here on Earth.

Free Choice

Yes, you are busy and some of that busyness is imposed on you by the choices you have made—to hold down a salaried job, to run a professional practice or business, to raise strong kids, to pursue a beloved hobby or pastime, to keep yourself healthy and strong, to romance your lover and travel together for shared adventures, to learn something new...

If you don't take anything else away from this book, know this: Our lives are not carved in stone. We have choices. We have options. We have the power to change no matter how hard it might seem. There's always a way, you just have to look for it.

Our choice may certainly lead us to make a dramatic change and sell our business, quit the stressful job, or other seemingly major change, yet we can choose the status quo, too. We can choose to carry on the way we always have, just accepting the way life pushes us around. We can choose to consciously create something different for ourselves, even when that means rowing upstream for a while. We can choose to reach and stretch far, far, far... or comfortably grab what has always been right in front of us (but that we ignored). We are highly adaptable and can pivot on a dime when it's required or desired. Life would be pretty boring on Earth without humans—and without choice!

Many a person has let go of a great-paying, high-stress job for something less anxiety-producing. Conversely, any number of people have pursued the stressful job because it brings deep personal satisfaction and they love to rise to the challenge. In both cases, what was sought was balance. Happiness-creating equilibrium is the key. Mental and emotional sanity and calm are major elements of a life lived in a great yin-yang balance.

Don't think about what you *want* so much as what you *choose* to have. Do you choose to share your life and experiences and discuss decisions with a loved one? Then you need the balance that allows you to be together in peaceful surround-ings! If you are chasing the clock, you are not finding that much vaunted "quality time" for each other.

Remember how the mind works—it will give you what you decide or choose to have, but withhold from you that which you want (because wanting something means you lack it, and the mind is content to continue to give you that lack). What do you decide to have? What do you choose to create?

Don't give up on yourself. Remember the Japanese saying telling you to get back up every time you fall. Remember that life only hurts if you don't get back up after a fall. Remember, it is only a failure if you quit instead of learning and moving forward again.

When you feel out of balance and stumble, pause and ask how you need to get up. Rise up gently or boldly. You are not a failure; what you attempted just didn't work out (but taught you a lesson nonetheless). That is our power: deciding, choosing to stand back up, to learn, and to walk forward again. Go back to your yin-yang goal setting to become more of who you wish to be.

"Having it all" is possible once you learn to balance and work in harmony to fulfill your ambitious dreams. Always remind yourself that finding balance in your life is a choice. You have tremendous potential. With soft and hard goals working in tandem to your benefit, you are a powerful creator of the life you choose to have.

How Can You Continue Your Journey With Me?

Your chapter doesn't end here nor does my work end here… Writing this book is just one of the many ways to translate my message. Helping you find a better balance between work and life, helping you better manage your day to day life, helping you realize the power you have as a strong, unstoppable ambitious woman is just the beginning of the journey.

It shouldn't end here.

Everything that I've talked about related to Goal-Setting is just the tip of the iceberg, there's so much more to this.

But I can't possibly write down everything in one single book, what I am able to do to is teach you about it through my three-day program.

It's a value-packed productivity course that will take everything I've taught in this book to the next level.

It contains a breakdown of the key steps we, ambitious women need to take in order to work at a more efficient level, to maximize our productivity, to fulfill our most ambitious business goals without sacrificing any parts of our personal lives - so we can find a greater balance between work vs life. Goal-setting is just the beginning and only 10% of the entire process…

This is something I've created with my younger self in mind, the stubborn, naive, workaholic entrepreneur. This was everything I wish I had learned early on in my entrepreneurship journey and now I'm giving it all back to you, so *you can have it all without losing it all.*

There is a way, I promise you that.

You can sign up for the free program by scanning the QR code or visit the link below:

https://theeambitiouswoman.com/3dayprogram

While the program is specifically catered to entrepreneurs, the overall content can be valuable to other industries as well.

Thank you for staying until the end and I can't wait to see what you will accomplish after you put down this book, I hope to see you on the other side after you join my program!

Much love,
Selina F.

9 781952 231087